the piranha book

an account of the ill-famed piranha fishes of the rivers of tropical south america

edited by dr. george s. myers

with contributions by the editor, dr. herbert r. axelrod, and the late harald schultz

© 1972 by T.F.H. Publications, Inc. Ltd.

ISBN 0-87666-133-9

Cover photograph by Dr. Herbert R. Axelrod.

Distributed in the U.S.A. by T.F.H. Publications, Inc., 211 West Sylvania Avenue, P.O. Box 27, Neptune City, N.J. 07753; in England by T.F.H. (Gt. Britain) Ltd., 13 Nutley Lane, Reigate, Surrey; in Canada to the book store and library trade by Clarke, Irwin & Company, Clarwin House, 791 St. Clair Avenue West, Toronto 10, Ontario; in Canada to the pet trade by Rolf C. Hagen Ltd., 3225 Sartelon Street, Montreal 382, Quebec; in Southeast Asia by Y.W. Ong, 9 Lorong 36 Geylang, Singapore 14; in Australia and the south Pacific by Pet Imports Pty. Ltd., P.O. Box 149, Brookvale 2100, N.S.W., Australia. Published by T.F.H. Publications, Inc. Ltd., The British Crown Colony of Hong Kong.

Contents

This page and opposite: head of a piranha captured during the Axelrod-Yepez Venezuelan Expedition of 1971. On this page, the mouth area is shown in its natural state; opposite, the lips have been cut back to reveal the dentition. Photos by Dr. Herbert R. Axelrod.

FOREWORD

Since it was first published in "The Aquarium Journal" in 1949, my *A Monograph on the Piranha* has been the principal non-technical source of information on these fishes. During the subsequent twenty-three years, considerable has been written on these fishes, most notably the booklet by the late Harald Schultz, in which he attempted to demonstrate that piranhas are not nearly as dangerous as they have been presumed to be.

The present book reprints both my monograph and Schultz's booklet, as well as a brief popular article of mine on the difficulties of piranha classification together with other material selected by the publisher, Dr. Herbert R. Axelrod. Finally, I have added a new section, written by myself in 1971, in which I have attempted to assess how dangerous piranhas really are.

GEORGE S. MYERS
Alexander Agassiz Visiting Professor
Museum of Comparative Zoology
Harvard University
Cambridge, Mass.
October, 1971.

*Appeared as two installments (February and March, 1949 issues of *The Aquarium Journal*) in Part V of "The Amazon and Its Fishes."

A Monograph on the Piranha*

By GEORGE S. MYERS

A fish only a foot long with teeth so sharp and jaws so strong that it can chop out a piece of flesh from a man or an alligator as neatly as a razor, or clip off a finger or a toe, bone and all, with the dispatch of a meat-cleaver! A fish afraid of nothing, which attacks any animal, whatever its size, like lightning! A fish which never attacks singly but always in schools of a hundred or a thousand! A fish which is actually attracted by splashing and commotion in the water! And a fish which, when it smells blood, turns into a raging demon! This is the piranha, feared as no other animal is feared throughout the whole length of South America.

The piranha is the most dangerous fish in the Amazon and perhaps in the world. That evil reputation has for a long time rested with the Great White Shark *(Carcharodon)*, but the swimmer menaced by that 30-foot man-eater usually has only one animal to fight off, and agility or a lucky poke in the eye of the great fish *might* save him. The swimmer menaced by a school of lightning-swift piranhas would have no such chance, for nothing he could do would drive them off once he had been attacked. Moreover, if we care to contemplate preferences in regard to the manner of meeting our end, most of us would choose the single snap of the shark instead of being chopped to pieces by a hundred razorlike sets of teeth!

Before World War I few outside of South America had ever heard of the piranha, but it is now listed as a good English word in American dictionaries (Barnhart, 1947; see references at end of the monograph). Other travellers had described the piranha, but it was Theodore Roosevelt (1914) who really introduced piranhas to the English-speaking public. The gruesome stories he repeated, especially one concerning a man who fell off his horse while fording a Brazilian river and was completely skeletonized by piranhas, made the world aware of the terrible nature of this fearsome fish. In the 1920's and 30's, the Amazonian aquarium-fish trade opened the

7

Dangerous Piranha Species

A black piranha,
probably *Serrasalmus niger*.
Photo by Dr. Herbert R. Axelrod.

Black piranha, *Serrasalmus niger*. Photo by K. Paysan.

A dangerous piranha. Photo by Dr. Herbert R. Axelrod.

way for the occasional importations of piranhas by our larger public aquaria, and the aquarium-fish literature spread knowledge of the fish still more widely. Piranhas have even figured as the method-of-exit of at least one victim in a modern detective novel!

In spite of the many references to the piranha in both popular and scientific literature, no one has ever attempted to give a really adequate account of both its habits and its classification—for those who have written on classification have written little on the habits, and most of those who have dilated upon habits have been woefully uninformed about classification. In fact, some of the fishes described and figured in the aquarium literature as piranhas are not piranhas at all, and the dictionary definition of piranha is misleading in that it includes many fishes which have never been and could not be called piranhas, simply because their diet is mostly vegetarian. No one author has ever straightened out these matters, or put all phases of the piranha's history together. That is what I have attempted to do.

TALES OF THE PIRANHA

One of the first published accounts of the piranha, and almost certainly the first published figure, was given by Marcgrave, in his great work on Brazilian natural history, printed at Amsterdam in 1648. He called the fish *piraya* or *piranha*, and since he was dealing entirely with the coastal part of Brazil then temporarily acquired from the Portuguese by the Dutch, he was probably dealing with the species of the Rio São Francisco. This, together with his figure, which was excellent for those days, places his fish as *Serrasalmus piraya*, so named in 1820 by Cuvier, who utilized the common name given by Marcgrave as the specific scientific name of the species.

Marcgrave's account contains the elements so common to later stories of the piranha—the sharp teeth, the ability to bite out a chunk of flesh "as one would cut it out with razor," the danger of being bitten if one enters the water or even puts a foot or hand in it, and the thirst for blood—all are there.

Marcgrave really describes the piranha twice, as two species, one of which he says differs from the other in the presence of an adipose fin and in the red color of the ventral part. Either his first specimen had accidentally lost the adipose or Marcgrave failed to note that small fin, and the fish was simply not in breeding colors. His figure shows an adipose fin. But Marcgrave also described a third smaller "white" species with a less obtuse snout, which he says "does not bite as much as the others." This is almost certainly the pirambeba of the River São Francisco, *Serrasalmus brandtii* Luetken.

One of the earliest known portraits of an Amazonian piranha. Unpublished painting made on the Amazon between 1783 and 1792 under the direction of Alexandre Rodrigues Ferreira, first zoological explorer of Amazonia. Courtesy of Museu Nacional, Rio de Janeiro.

The earliest account that I can find of the piranha in Brazil, but one which was not printed until 1825, is that of Gabriel Soares de Sousa, in his *Descriptive Treatise on Brazil in 1587*. In Chapter 144, he says (my own translation from the Portuguese): "Piranha, that is to say, scissors; it is a fish of the great rivers, and where they are, they are many; it is of the kind of the Sargus but larger and in color very silvered; this fish is very fat and palatable and takes the line (hook); but has such teeth that they cut the hook at the root; because of which the Indians do not trust themselves to the water where this fish is; because they attack them much and bite them cruelly; they attack the genitals and cut them off (when the Indians) go hunting and cross the rivers where these fish swim."

The great Von Humboldt, who travelled in Spanish America in the 1790's, and whose sumptuous folio volumes on his travels did so much to make Spanish America known to the world, devotes two pages to the piranha (caribe) of Venezuela and its vicious habits. In fact, almost every traveller who has visited the haunts of this terrible fish has had something to say about it. In the South American travel books in any well-stocked library

One of the dangerous piranhas, probably *Serrasalmus nattereri*. Photo by H. Hansen, Aquarium Berlin.

Head of the "red piranha," *Serrasalmus nattereri,* with the lips cut away to show the teeth. Photo by Dr. Herbert R. Axelrod.

one will find gruesome tales of the piranha by the score, but as time and books pass by, later writers have more to choose from, and the accounts become more gory. Few of these are of much literary merit, since the authors in their revulsion (or fascination), rush from horror to horror with increasing speed.

The least hair-raising allusion is perhaps that of Jose Verissimo, the well-known Brazilian litterateur of two generations ago. In his little book of 1895 on Amazonian fishing, he says: ". . . place a shot or an arrow in the right spot and (the alligator) falls into the water, blood pouring from his body. Then there flashes to the surface, famished and voracious, clouds of fluviatile devils, obstinate and bloodthirsty—the piranhas! Even the bullet-proof hide cannot resist these strong, razor-sharp teeth."

Couto de Magalhães, a modern Brazilian writer, has many piranha tales, including some of the apocryphal ones which commonly circulate in Brazil. But the following is only too true: "In the historical documents on the war between Brazil and Paraguay, there are several references to tragic cases of soldiers who, wounded and obliged by the enemy to ford the creeks or rivers of that region, were quickly killed by piranhas, leaving only their white skeletons on the bottom of the transparent waters of the streams."

Many are the stories of persons who have lost fingers and toes by carelessly trailing them over the sides of canoes, and some of these cases have concerned zoologists who should have known better. One instance even happened in the United States. In 1934 or 1935, when Fred Orsinger was in charge of the Department of Commerce Aquarium in Washington, he acquired two half-grown piranhas, apparently *Serrasalmus nattereri*. He was proudly showing me these fishes one day and took the cover off the four-foot aquarium in which the fish were kept so that I could see them from above. For some reason or other he flicked his finger on the surface of the water.

"You'd better watch out, Fred," I warned him. "Those fishes may take off the end of your finger."

Fred looked down at the fish and replied, "Oh, I'm careful!"

A couple of weeks later Fred lost a piece of the end of his finger to one of those same fishes—while flicking the surface of the water! The wound wasn't bad. Fred was lucky. But he didn't flick the surface of *that* tank any more!

In the cattle country of Matto Grosso, in the Rio Paraguay basin of south-western Brazil, piranhas are a scourge. They not rarely cut the teats off the udders of the cows, and once there is blood in the water, no animal is safe. In driving herds across rivers or creeks, many cattle are lost, and it is said that the cattlemen expect to lose at least one steer at each major crossing.

Although piranhas are caught for food almost everywhere they occur, strong tackle must be used to catch them. All who have fished for them agree that they can cut off the shank of a thin steel hook, or a copper leader, with one snap. But their mouths are small, and heavy but small long-shanked hooks, and heavy phosphor-bronze or light chain leaders are recommended. They are said to bite well when the bait is bright red, even if it is only a piece of cloth, but they are also taken with bait of small dough balls. Hartley says they were most numerous and could always be caught in relatively quiet water, where a sandbank, or the bank of the stream, shelved off steeply into deep water. They have a hard roof to the mouth and must be sharply hooked when they bite.

Fresh-caught piranhas in the boat are always dangerous, for they flip about and snap at anything near them. They can take a piece out of the end of a paddle, or a shoe with the toe inside, with ease. In many parts of the world it is common practice of fishermen to hold a fresh-caught fish between the teeth, while rebaiting the hook or doing something else with the hands. General Rondon, the great Brazilian explorer, tells of the case of one of his assistants, Lieutenant Pyrineus, who tried this with a piranha (see Rondon, p. 300):

"He put some sticks of dynamite above a rapids, and got some curimbatas, piavas, and piranhas. He secured one of the latter in his mouth to hold it, while he picked up other fishes. He was then bitten, the piranha taking out a large piece of his tongue, producing a strong hemorrhage, which nearly suffocated him."

We could go on with such stories interminably, but those who wish to follow up the bloody literature of the piranha may easily find plenty of reading matter. The fullest accounts known to me, all of which are cited in the bibliography at the end of this article, are those by the following authors: Allen (in Eigenmann and Allen), Eigenmann, Hartt, Hartley, Roth, Cutright, and Theodore Roosevelt. All of these are in English and nearly all give many references to still other writers. The best accounts I know of in Portuguese are those of Ihering (1934 and 1940) and Magalhães. Brehm gives one in German. If one reads other languages, he needs only to look up books in those languages by travellers in piranha country.

Finally, it is interesting to note how widely the name piranha is used in Brazil, which includes the bulk of the range of these beasts. In 1899, Moreira Pinto, in his great geographical dictionary of Brazil, lists 24 towns, rivers, mountains and such geographical locations called Piranha or Piranhas.

GENERAL CLASSIFICATION OF THE PIRANHAS

The piranhas—for there are several species of them—belong to the characin or characid family, technically known as Characidae, a large group of fresh-water fishes native to tropical America and Africa. The largest

Male (above) and female of a dangerous piranha species spawned at the Cincinnati Zoo. Photos by Dr. Herbert R. Axelrod.

Six-month-old juvenile, one of the offspring of piranhas that spawned at the Cincinnati Zoo. Photo by Dr. Herbert R. Axelrod.

A very large adult of *Serrasalmus nattereri*, the most widespread species of the dangerous piranhas. Photo by Dr. Herbert R. Axelrod.

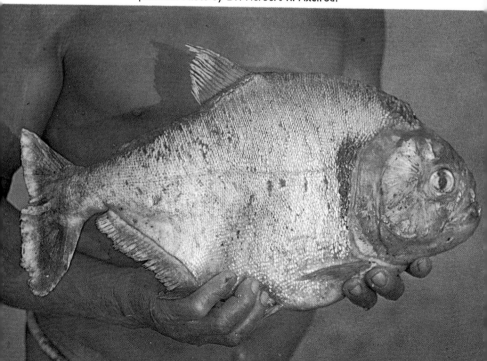

members of the family are the great tigerfish *(Hydrocynus goliath)* of the Congo River, which is known to attain 83 pounds and said to reach 150, and the dourado *(Salminus brasiliensis)* of southern Brazil, which is commonly caught up to 45 pounds and is thought to reach 65 or more. However, most members of the characin family are smaller, and the adult length of the species would probably average not more than 6 or 8 inches. The smallest ones scarcely reach an inch in length.

The characins are divided into few or many subfamilies according to the authority followed, but only that part of the classification which affects the piranhas needs to be considered here. Eigenmann (1915) studied the characins having a serrated abdominal edge and grouped them in two subfamilies, the Serrasalminae and the Mylinae, the former carnivorous and with a single row of teeth in each jaw, the latter herbivorous and with two rows of teeth in the upper jaw and sometimes also in the lower. Norman (1929) united these two groups into one, which he called Serrasalmoninae. Nomenclaturally speaking, Norman's subfamily term Serrasalmoninae is incorrect, and Eigenmann's is correct, so we should spell the subfamily name Serrasalminae in any case. And it matters very little ichthyologically whether we unite or separate these two subfamilies, except that "piranha" has been defined as a member of the subfamily Serrasalminae. If one follows Eigenmann, this definition is partly correct, but if we follow Norman, it errs most egregiously. Having studied these fishes myself, and being familiar with the reasons behind this difference of emphasis by Eigenmann and Norman, I believe Norman's arrangement is better, and unite both the carnivorous and herbivorous groups into one subfamily, Serrasalminae. The group is confined to South America east of the Andes.

The vegetarian Serrasalminae consist of nine or ten genera and between 50 and 60 species. All are deep-bodied, flattened fishes, and are known almost everywhere by the common name *pacu* (pronounced pah-koo, with the accent on the second syllable). The largest ones are food fishes reaching a limit of about 44 pounds in weight, which run upstream during the period of high water and spawn when they have reached impassable rapids or falls. They lurk in the water under overhanging trees, the fruit of which is one of their especial foods. The Indians know this well, and shoot the pacu with arrows after calling them to the surface by dropping fruit into the water. It is said that the clearing away of these native fruit trees from above the banks of rivers in settled regions has caused the extinction of pacu in many places.

The carnivorous Serrasalminae include the piranhas. They have been placed in three or four genera, but as Norman has demonstrated, not more than two are worthy of recognition. *Pygopristis* contains a single species found in the Amazon and the Guianas, but not much is known about its habits. The second genus is that of the piranhas, *Serrasalmus*, and there are

The most dangerous of the Amazonian piranhas (*Serrasalmus nattereri*). Watercolor sketch from life, made at Villa Bella in January 1866 by J. Burckhardt, under the direction of Louis Agassiz.

Head of a black piranha, *Serrasalmus niger*. Photo by Dr. Herbert R. Axelrod.

A *Serrasalmus* species, possibly *S. nattereri*. Photo by Dr. Karl Knaack.

at least 17 or 18 distinct species, *but only four of these are true piranhas.* That is, only four of the species are really known to be dangerous to man, and these are the only species invariably known as *piranha* in Brazil.

TEETH OF THE PIRANHA

The teeth and jaws with which the piranha can do such execution have been described many times, and are excellently figured by Eigenmann (1915), so we need not give too long a description. The jaws of the most dangerous species are short and broad, and the lower one is deep and powerful. The teeth are triangular in form, with an acute median point and very sharp edges, and each bears a small but sharp-edged cusp on the posterior side. This cusp is usually in line with the anterior sharp edge of the succeeding tooth, and blends with its profile, so that the row of teeth looks, in profile, like a continuous saw-edge with the small cusp of each tooth not showing. In fact, this palisade of sharpened teeth does practically form a continuous sawlike cutting edge in each jaw.

There is only one row of teeth in each jaw and they are sharper than almost any shark teeth. When the piranha snaps these teeth together, the points in the upper row fit into the notches of the lower row, and the power of the jaw muscles is such that there is scarcely any living substance save the hardest ironwood that will not be clipped off.

Unlike the teeth of most predaceous fishes, the teeth of the piranha are not adapted to lacerate, crush, mangle, or seize and hold the prey. There are not several rows of teeth in each jaw as in many sharks. There is but one, and this is adapted only for *clipping off* small pieces of the prey, which in some instances is much larger than the fish itself, but is probably smaller most of the time.

The best mechanical imitation of piranha teeth and jaws, and a very good imitation indeed, is a bear-trap, but one with the teeth so sharpened on the edges, and the spring so strong, that they would clip off the bear's foot instead of merely holding it.

The mouth of the piranha is small. The size of the average piece bitten off would be that of a large olive or nutmeg. The pieces are swallowed whole, and rapidly, and the fish snaps many times.

THE NAME OF THE PIRANHA

First off, let's pronounce the name right. It is not "piranna," as most English-speaking people tend to mispronounce it. While more on this subject is given further on, we should learn right now that the proper pronunciation is close to the English "peer-on-yah." Is that too hard to say?

The name *piranha* is from the great general South American Indian language called Tupi-Guarani (pronounced too-pee gwah-rah-nee, the accent in each word on the last syllable), which is widespread in Brazil and from which are derived most of the common names of animals and plants used today in Brazil. It is interesting that the Portuguese settlers in Brazil, although retaining Portuguese as their language, adopted Indian terms much more widely than did the English settlers in North America. If we had done this, our vocabulary of common names for North American fishes would not be as poor as it is, and we would not be forced to use pike, perch, bream, and smelt for many totally unrelated fishes.

By a seemingly strange coincidence, the name for common household scissors along the Amazon is *piranha*. Now a number of writers, including even such a philologist as Burton (1869), who translated the epic Portuguese poetry of Camões and rendered the *Arabian Nights* into English from the Arabic, have said that the fish name piranha means simply *scissors*. This is most misleading, as Hartt (1870) has plainly shown, but no author or dictionary (English or Portuguese) that I happen to have seen has given the complete derivation of the word correctly. Cutright (1940) came nearest, but got his spelling wrong.

The *patois* spoken along the Amazon is a hybrid language formed mostly of Tupi with some Portuguese and other elements added. It is called the *Lingua Geral* (General Tongue or Language) in Brazil, and Stradelli's dictionary of it (1929) is very complete. In this Lingua Geral, *pira* means fish, and modifying terms are joined to it to form the names of particular kinds. For example, the leaf-fish *(Monocirrhus)* is *pira-caa* (pee-rah-kah-ah, with the accent on the last syllable), meaning "fish-leaf."

According to Stradelli, the word for tooth is *ranha*, *tanha*, or *sanha*, depending on the local dialect, so it is easy to see that piranha means "fish-tooth" or "toothed-fish." But why scissors should be called the same thing is another story. The fish was not named from the instrument, but the reverse. The name piranha was in use by the Indians long before they ever saw a pair of scissors. From prehistoric times, down even to the present, each Amazonian or Guiana Indian has kept about him, in his camp or dangling from his g-string or arrow-quiver, the jaw of a piranha, the sharp teeth of which are used for a knife-and-scissors combined, to cut bark, thongs, his own hair, wood, or anything. Hartley, Allen, and many other authors say the modern Guiana Indians use them to cut the tips of poisoned blowgun darts almost through, just before using, so that the tip will break off after entering the prey. What is more natural than for the Indians, when presented with scissors by the white man, to call them piranha?

Piranha is pronounced peer-on-ya or, more correctly, pee-rahn-yah, with the accent on the "rahn" and the "r" very faintly rolled. The whole word is formed in the front of the mouth with the tongue kept to the teeth (which method of pronunciation, if remembered and followed, will help most Americans to pronounce Spanish and Portuguese better than they do).

Two species of piranhas are represented in this catch; with living piranhas (or even with piranhas that are not definitely known to be dead), it's a good idea to keep one's fingers away from those efficient teeth. Photo by Dr. Herbert R. Axelrod.

A sagittal (down the middle) section of a piranha, to show the interior. The two large white organs in the upper part of the body cavity are the two sections of the air-bladder, with the coiled intestine below. Photo by Dr. Herbert R. Axelrod.

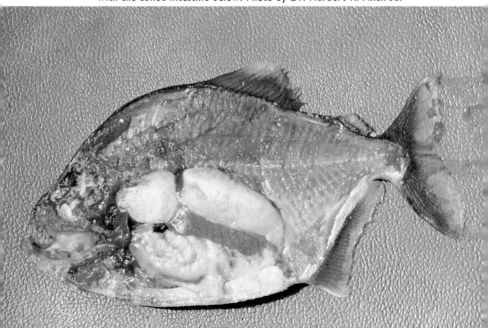

A species showing a distinctive pattern of markings. Photo by Dr. Herbert R. Axelrod.

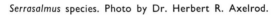

Serrasalmus species. Photo by Dr. Herbert R. Axelrod.

Now it is generally recognized in Brazil that there are dangerous piranhas and nondangerous piranhas, and terms are in use to distinguish them. But in Brazil, as elsewhere, the meanings of names are determined not by professors but by general usage, and usage of the common names of animals differs from region to region. The application of any one name is more or less loose. Those who wish an especially fine example need only search out thoroughly the usage of the terms *pike* and *pickerel* in North America, as Mr. A. C. Weed did a few years ago, or of the English term *perch*.

In a loose way, any Brazilian (and I do not mean a city dweller who never catches a fish) in almost any part of Brazil where these fishes are found is likely to call any fish of the genus *Serrasalmus* or *Pygopristis* a "piranha," when you show him one. But if you pin him down, he is likely to hedge, unless the fish is plainly and unmistakably one of the kinds dangerous to man. If it is a dangerous one, and he knows his local fishes, he will tell you flatly that the fish is a piranha. If it is one of the inoffensive kinds, he will give it another name right off, or will at least qualify the term piranha by some adjective, or tell you the fish is not a "piranha-verdadeira" (true piranha). In the interior of the state of Minas Gerais, or in most parts of the great chunk of eastern Brazil which bulges out into the Atlantic (that is, some third of the country), the inoffensive species of *Serrasalmus* are called *pirambeba* (pee-ram-bay-ba, with the accent on the "bay"). According to Hartt (1870, p. 403, who calls it pirampeba), this name is compounded of the Tupi words *piranha* and *peba*, meaning "flat." This is probably true, although Stradelli gives *pema* rather than peba as the equivalent of "flat" in the Lingua Geral, the difference in the consonants being probably a matter of dialect. Actually, the letters p, b, and v are pronounced much alike in some parts of Brazil. The truth is that the more innocuous species of *Serrasalmus* are considerably more compressed, both in head and in body, than the dangerous ones, and Hartt's pirampeba, like Marcgrave's third form of piranha, is probably *Serrasalmus brandtii* Luetken.

The adjectives that are commonly added to the word piranha usually but not always denote color, and the usage of such terms is confused. *Piranha vermelha* (red piranha), *piranha preta* (black piranha), or *piranha cachorra* (dog piranha), where used, certainly almost always refer to the dangerous kinds. *Piranha branca* (white piranha) is almost always applied to inoffensive species, *Serrasalmus rhombeus* or *S. brandtii*, which are widely distributed and very common and are called pirambeba in northeastern Brazil. *Piranha mapara* (with accent on the terminal "a") is said always to refer to *Pygopristis*. (See Von Ihering, 1940.)

Thus it may be seen that the name piranha cannot be applied with equal force and correctness to all the species of carnivorous Serrasalminae. Moreover, the man-eating species are the only ones to which the name is invariably applied by those whose common usage of the term determines its meaning—

26

the people of Brazil. We may, therefore, define the word piranha as follows: certain species of South American fresh-water fishes of the family Characidae, genus *Serrasalmus*, dangerous to man; loosely, any carnivorous member of the subfamily Serrasalminae.

The only really distinctive name for the more inoffensive species of *Serrasalmus* is pirambeba, mentioned above, and if we wish an English name for these fishes, this term, like piranha, might be used.

The term *piraya*, mentioned as an alternative name of these beasts by Marcgrave in 1648, does not even appear in Von Ihering's great dictionary of Brazilian animals (1940). However, Burton (1869, vol. 2, p. 33) says that piraya (spelled by him pirayya) is a common corruption of piranha in the states of Minas and São Paulo.

There are other names besides piranha and pirambeba applied to species of *Serrasalmus* in Brazil. *Chupita* is sometimes used for the dangerous forms, and *rodoleira* is a name applied to some species, in northeastern Brazil (see Von Ihering, 1940).

In Spanish-speaking Venezuela, the common, dangerous piranha is almost invariably called *caribe* (pronounced cah-ree-bay, with accent on the second syllable), while the same species is called *palometa* (pah-loh-may-ta, accent on the "may") in Bolivia and other Spanish-speaking parts of the Rio Paraguay and Rio Paraná basins. These names are of interesting derivation. The Caribs, or Caribes, were a warlike and cruel Indian people who were indigenous to northern South America and who had, at the time of Columbus, recently spread through most of the West Indies, subjugating the gentler tribes who had preceded them. The application of the name to the fish is obvious. The term palometa is applied widely in Spanish America to sea fishes of the jack family (Carangidae). It means "little dove" and may have been applied ironically to the piranha but more likely came into use because of the general similarity of shape to the marine jacks. Devincenzi and Teague, for illustration, call the piranha *palometa de rio* (palometa of the river) to distinguish it from *palometa de mar* (palometa of the sea).

Through a transposition of terms difficult to understand but which is scarcely unique in the history of the common names of fishes, the term piranha (or pirana) is restricted to one of the less dangerous species on the middle Rio Uruguay, where the deadly species is called palometa, as in Bolivia (see Devincenzi and Teague).

Alexander von Humboldt, quoting the account of Alonzo de Herera's expedition of 1535, by Fray Pedro Simon, says that the piranha was there called *caribito*, or "little caribe." Humboldt himself says that the Maipures Indians of the Orinoco called the fish *umati* and that a Parageni Indian called it *bahumehi*. Both Up de Graf (1923, p. 68) and Allen (in Eigenmann and Allen, 1942, p. 242) report that paña (pronounced pahn-yah, with accent on

Less Dangerous Piranhas, or Pirambebas

One of the less dangerous species of *Serrasalmus*, called pirambeba. Photo by Dr. Herbert R. Axelrod.

A trio of one of the pirambeba species. Photo by Dr. Herbert R. Axelrod.

first syllable) is the commonly used name in Amazonian Peru. Schomburgk (1843) gives the following names for several species of *Serrasalmus* in Guiana (the name of the Indian tribe using each name given in parentheses): *arri* (Macusi) *katte* (Macusi; the same fish called *chitão* in Lingua Geral), *huma* (Arawak), *arai* (Macusi), and *pirai* (Carib). The last three names are said to pertain to the same species, *Serrasalmus niger* Schomburgk. According to Castelnau (1855, p. 72) the Chavantes Indians call the piranha *coicoa* (the "o" and "i" pronounced separately), and the Carajas call it *djuta*.

The Carib name *pirai*, and its variant spelling *perai* (pronounced pereye), is the name current today for the most dangerous piranhas in British Guiana (see Hartley, 1917; Roth, 1943). It is easy to see that this name is closely related to piranha, though perhaps less so than it seems. Some writers indicate that the "a" and "i" are separately pronounced (per-ah-ee) and not as a diphthong.

THE DANGEROUS SPECIES

Four species of *Serrasalmus* are always dangerous to man. These differ from the more inoffensive ones not only in the usually somewhat greater size but also in the broader and much blunter head, the much heavier and apparently slightly shorter lower jaw, and the thicker (less compressed) body. Two of these species, *S. piraya* of the Rio São Francisco and *S. ternetzi* of the Rio Paraguay, have a muzzle so blunt that there is only a very slight concavity in the profile above the eyes, if any at all. *S. nattereri* of the Orinoco, Amazon, and Paraguay-Parana systems normally has a slight concavity in the profile at this place, while *S. niger* of the Guiana region has a deeper concavity and narrower head, thus approaching the appearance of the more innocuous forms.

In size these dangerous species appear to differ from each other, but it must be remembered that there are comparatively few records of exact measurements of any except museum specimens and these are usually smaller individuals, simply because scientific collectors usually select specimens which will fit into their containers of preservative. Many writers refer to piranhas generally as attaining the "size of a man's hand" but all of the dangerous species and some of the others grow much larger. It is quite true that many schools of "hand-size" piranhas are seen, but these are probably all smaller, younger fish. Like other fishes, piranhas form schools of individuals of approximately equal size.

Two of the forms appear to grow larger than the others. *Serrasalmus piraya*, which is found only in the Rio São Francisco, commonly reaches at least 20 United States inches (51 cm.) in total length, and is therefore the largest and most dangerous species. *S. niger* of Guiana reaches at least 14½ inches since the type specimen in the Berlin Museum is that long (365 millimeters). The largest measured example on record known positively to be

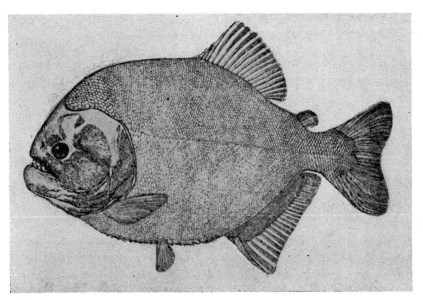

The largest and most deadly of the piranhas, *Serrasalmus piraya* of the River Sao Francisco in eastern Brazil. Grows to 2 feet in length. After Luetken.

S. nattereri is the 27-cm. (10½-inch) example in the British Museum. *S. ternetzi* of the Rio Paraguay reaches almost 10 inches. Probably all of these four species sometimes grow from 2 to 4 inches longer than the above records would indicate.

Formerly the dangerous piranhas were arrayed in three genera *(Pygocentrus, Gastropristis,* and *Rooseveltiella)* (see Eigenmann, 1915) distinct from *Serrasalmus,* but Norman places all of them in one genus, *Serrasalmus,* and it is my considered opinion that valid generic lines cannot be drawn within this grouping. However, the four dangerous species might be placed in a separate subgenus, *Pygocentrus,* which is poorly defined by the broader head and the very short distance between the adipose fin and the dorsal fin. One of the less dangerous forms has been kept by all modern ichthyologists in a separate genus, *Pygopristis,* because of its crenulate teeth. Parenthetically, it should be stated that this generic name has been spelled *Serrasalmo* by most authors, but Lacépède, the original proposer of the name, spelled it *Serrasalmus* in 1803 and the International Rules of Nomenclature require that the original form be accepted.

Serrasalmus piraya Cuvier is the species of the basin of the Rio São Francisco in eastern Brazil, is not found elsewhere, and is the only species of the *Pygocentrus*-type found in that river. I have never seen it alive, since,

31

Pacu Species, Mostly Vegetarians

A species of the genus *Colossoma*, one of the genera of larger pacus. Photo by Dr. Herbert R. Axelrod.

An adult "silver dollar" pacu of the genus *Metynnis*. Fishes of no other genus of characins have the long, low adipose fin (on the back between the dorsal fin and the tail) characteristic of *Metynnis*, but the several species of this genus are difficult to identify. Photo by Dr. Herbert R. Axelrod.

when I was at the great rapids of the São Francisco at Pirapora, no piranhas were there. The local fishermen said that the fish had retired downstream and were caught at Piraporà only at the time of high water. We seined in the river and in tributaries near Pirapora and never saw a piranha. This species differs from all the others in uniformly possessing well-developed rays in the adipose fin, a peculiarity very rare among fishes which have this fin. It is also the largest and most dangerous species. Hartt, whose personal observations are unimpeachable, saw them himself up to 20 inches long, and the fishermen told him they grow to 24. Luetken, the eminent Danish ichthyologist, had one specimen caught from the Rio das Velhas, of 17 Danish inches (about 18 U.S. or English inches). It is fortunate that only one river basin is plagued by such a beast. Piranhas over half a meter long must be fearsome creatures!

Serrasalmus ternetzi Steindachner is a very blunt-headed species (agreeing in this with the preceding), known only from the Rio Paraguay in northern Argentina, Paraguay, and presumably in southwestern Brazil and the Rio Paraná. Probably it is common, but there is little on record concerning it, probably because the natives do not distinguish it from the common species. It differs from the following species by the blunter head and the shorter distance between the dorsal fin and the adipose. The largest recorded example is just under 10 inches in total length.

Serrasalmus nattereri Kner is the most widespread species of true piranha and is undoubtedly the one that has figured in most of the human fatalities reported. It is found throughout the basin of the Orinoco in Venezuela, the rivers of Guiana, the Amazon basin, and the Paraná and Paraguay basins clear to Argentina. It is not found in the S. Francisco or in any of the coastal rivers in southeastern Brazil. (The latter are, fortunately, free of piranhas.) This fish has a slightly less blunt and "bulldog-shaped" muzzle than the preceding species, and there is often a very faint concavity in the profile of the head above the eyes. Occasional examples have fairly well developed rays in the adipose fin. The colors of fresh-caught fish, especially males at or near the breeding season, are very bright, for the sides show much metallic blue and the underside of the head and the belly are smeared with brilliant red. Because of this the fish is often called *piranha vermelha* (see above). Presumably the same color is found in the two preceding species. The distance between the dorsal and adipose fins goes about twice in the basal length of the dorsal fin. This is a smaller species, the largest recorded example known to me being $10\frac{1}{2}$ inches (27 cm.) in total length.

Serrasalmus niger Schomburgk is a very little known species of British Guiana. In fact the only authentic specimen known to science is the original type example preserved in the Berlin Museum. Eigenmann (1915) and Norman (1929) give the characteristics of this fish from the Berlin specimen, and the latter mentions one in the Paris Museum supposed to be the same species. The strange shape of the Berlin specimen is probably due to deformation, since it is stuffed and dried. But Norman and others have overlooked Hartley's article of 1917, in which he discusses what he says is this species, and gives photographs of it from Guiana specimens. If Hartley was right in his identification, this species is common not only in Guiana but also in the Rio Negro in northern Brazil, whence I have examined specimens. It is, in fact, the *piranha negra* of the Rio Negro, differing from all others in its smoky yellowish-brown to blackish color, with golden reflections on the scales. There is a distinct but slight concavity in the profile above the eyes, and the distance between adipose and dorsal fin is nearly equal to the base-length of the latter. Moreover, the lower lobe of the tail-fin is considerably larger than the upper, a characteristic seen in some other species of *Serrasalmus*. This species seems to mark a transition between the very blunt-nosed *Pygocentrus*-type of piranha and the more sharp-nosed, less dangerous kinds. But *niger* is a dangerous fish, as Hartley shows, although it is not at all certain that his account of the habits (one of the best published) does not apply in part to the preceding species *(S. nattereri)*, which is found in Guiana, but to which he does not refer. This species grows to 14 inches or more in total length. The range may be much wider than is known, since "black piranhas" are reported from several places in the Amazon basin.

THE OTHER PIRANHAS, OR PIRAMBEBAS

In discussing native names I have referred to "dangerous" and "inoffensive" piranhas. These divisions are generally recognized in regions where piranhas occur, but it must not be supposed that these are exact, scientifically proved groupings. The trouble is that when a man is bitten in the water he either does not live to tell of it or at least can seldom be sure of the scientific identity of the species concerned, even if he is an ichthyologist. However, from the stories of persons who have seen piranhas devouring animals, or have caught them extensively, we are certain that the "*Pygocentrus*-type" species are the villains in most instances, and there are no records whatever which definitely implicate any of the other species in human fatalities. This does not mean that none of the other species is ever dangerous, even though in certain places certain species are well known never to attack swimmers. It is my impression that any species of *Serrasalmus* might attack and destroy a swimmer if he were wounded and there were blood in the water. With this preamble, we may proceed to consider the other species.

These are the *pirambebas*, almost everywhere considered harmless. They all have narrower heads, more flattened (laterally compressed) bodies, and more projecting, sharper muzzles than the deadlier forms. They form a graded series from larger species somewhat similar to *S. niger* (which is the most "pirambeba-like" of the dangerous ones) to relatively elongate, sharp-

Metynnis species, one of the smaller "silver dollar" pacus. Note the long, low adipose fin, which is always diagnostic of the genus *Metynnis*. Photo by Dr. Herbert R. Axelrod.

A species of *Metynnis*. Photo by Dr. Herbert R. Axelrod.

Young of unidentified species of pacu. Photo by Dr. Herbert R. Axelrod.

snouted fishes such as *S. rhombeus* and *S. elongatus.* Norman's monograph lists 13 species of this type, but the classification of a few is still doubtful, and more species may eventually be recognized. In addition I have examples of an unnamed new species from the Rio Negro. It will serve no purpose to treat all the species here, since Norman's monograph may be consulted. Only the commoner or more striking ones are mentioned.

Pygopristis denticulatus (Cuvier), the so-called *piranha-mapará,* differs from all the other species of *Serrasalmus* in the crenulated (5-cusped) teeth. It is unlikely that it ever attacks man, but it is widely distributed in the Amazon, the Guianas, and probably Venezuela. It grows to 8 or 9 inches.

Serrasalmus brandtii Luetken is the pirambeba, piranha branca, or piranha de lagoa of the Rio São Francisco basin. It is very similar to the preceding species but lacks the dark caudal marking. Apparently this and *S. piraya* are the only species of the genus in the S. Francisco basin. I have bathed in Lagoa Santa, where this species is common, and natives say it is harmless.

A pacu, vegetarian relative of the piranha. Note that the lower jaw does not project. Painting made under direction of Alexandre Rodrigues Ferreira, early Portuguese scientific explorer of the Amazon (1783–1792) whose valuable manuscripts and paintings have never been published. Courtesy of Museu Nacional, Rio de Janeiro.

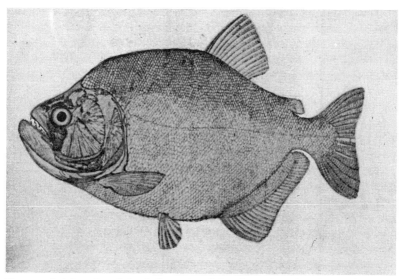

The so-called harmless "piranha" or pirambeba, *Serrasalmus brandtii* of the River Sao Francisco in eastern Brazil, to show differences in form from dangerous species. After Luetken.

Serrasalmus spilopleura Kner differs from other species in the dark band across the terminal part of the tail-fin, and is found all the way from Venezuela and the Guianas throughout the Amazon basin and southward in the interior to Buenos Aires in Argentina. It grows to about 10 inches and is probably not a dangerous form, although personally I would not like to trust it too far.

Serrasalmus rhombeus (Linnaeus) is the commonest species of the genus in the Amazon basin, in Guiana, and in the Orinoco. It is more elongate in form than the others, is certainly of very little danger to man, and grows to about 1 foot in total length. It swarms throughout the Amazon and the Guiana rivers.

Serrasalmus elongatus Kner is the most elongate of all the species, the depth of the body going about 2.6 times in the length from snout-tip to end of lateral line. It is very doubtful that it ever attacks man, although it probably reaches 8 or 10 inches in length.

The other species are in general less well known than these.

GENERAL DISTRIBUTION OF PIRANHAS

The genera *Serrasalmus* and *Pygopristis* are apparently quite absent in the following South American waters: (1) all stream basins emptying into the

Enlarged view of the head of *Colossoma nigripinnis*. Photo by Dr. Herbert R. Axelrod.

A young pacu of the genus *Myloplus*. Photo by Dr. Herbert R. Axelrod.

Mylossoma aureum, one of the "silver dollar" pacus other than *Metynnis*. Photo by Dr. Herbert R. Axelrod.

Pacific, (2) the basin of the Rio Magdalena in Colombia, (3) the basin of Lake Maracaibo and all the short coastal streams between it and the delta of the Orinoco, (4) the streams flowing directly into the Atlantic from southernmost Bahia state in Brazil south to eastern Uruguay, (5) most or all of the drainages south of the Rio de la Plata estuary streams in Argentina, and (6) probably all streams at an altitude of 2000 feet or more. Remember that the word "rio" means "river"—in either Spanish or Portuguese—when looking at a map of Latin America.

The presence of piranhas in the isolated drainages of west-central Argentina is not known. North of the Rio São Francisco, many of the coastal streams around the "bulge" of Brazil contain *Serrasalmus*, especially those in Ceará and Maranhão, but they may be absent in some of the more southerly ones of this area.

So far as I have been able to find, there is no stream basin which has the more innocuous species and not the dangerous ones, or vice versa. Everywhere they occur, at least two species seem to be present, and in the Amazon and to the northward, and in the streams forming the Plata basin, several forms exist.

HABITS

It must be pointed out again that little is on record concerning particular species, and that most writers who speak of piranhas are referring solely to the more dangerous ones, but without bothering to distinguish the species. What can be said of habits, then, refers almost wholly to the true, deadly piranhas.

All seem to agree that piranhas do not occur in the swift waters of rapids. They prefer quieter places and deep pools, and from Hartley's account, they would seem to keep near the bottom.

They occur in what have been called schools, but brief observations made on a large tank containing about ten adults of two or three species in the Shedd Aquarium in Chicago lead me to believe that their schooling behavior is rather strongly modified by their fear of each other.

Breder's account of *Astyanax* in Panama shows that these small characins, like so many other predatory fishes, will immediately tear up and devour any injured member of the school. Piranhas behave in this way. The piranhas in the tank in Chicago all showed regenerated semicircles in the fins where they had bitten each other, and wild-caught fish show the same. The captive fishes swam slowly about, each keeping well away from its fellows and showing a plain desire not to have another directly behind it, where the neighbor could attack unseen. It is wholly probable that exactly the same tactics are followed in wild schools. After all, each fish is possessed of a weapon—the teeth—which can deal sudden death to any other member of the school, and they reminded me strongly of a set of ruthless gunmen, each with a pistol in his pocket and each one quite mindful that all the rest were ready to use them at any moment.

When food appears, the others are almost forgotten and the whole school flashes savagely at the prey, chopping off pieces and swallowing in a swirl of darting fishes. It is probably at this time above all others that the hungry fishes, in a cloud of blood and juices from the food, most frequently bite each other, probably more by accident than for other reasons. But a member of the school so unlucky as to be seriously bitten by another is attacked by the rest with gusto and he soon disappears. I realize that some writers say piranhas do not attack each other, but this is certainly not true.

It has been noted by several writers (Hartley, Hartt, etc.) that piranhas never go into brackish or salt waters. Like the other members of the Characidae, they are strictly fresh-water fishes.

From my observations at Pirapora on the Rio São Francisco, where piranhas were not present just previous to the rains and high water, and were said by the fishermen to come upstream with the rising of the river, it would seem that these fishes are migratory to some degree. It is known that the larger species of pacú ascend the rivers to spawn, and it would seem likely that their close relatives the piranhas do so. However, I have found no mention of the piranha being migratory in any of the numerous accounts of this fish, and no mention is made by Brazilian authors of piranhas taking part in the great annual fish-run, or *piracema* (pee-rah-say-ma; accent on the "say"), which occurs in most Brazilian rivers when the water rises. This subject needs investigation.

I have found four accounts of the breeding habits of the piranha. Holder (1883) published a figure of a "hanging nest of the perai"—a coconut-like object floating on the water, loosely suspended from a palm tree, guarded by two fishes. But Gill (1907, p. 436), who asked Holder where he got his information, was told that Holder had forgotten. I think we too may forget the matter.

Cutright (1940) quotes from a book by C. B. Brown *(Canoe and Camp Life in British Guiana, 1877)*, which I have not seen. Brown says the eggs he saw were laid on submerged plants and matted roots just beneath the surface near the bank of a stream. His Indians told Brown the two adult piranhas present were the parents watching the eggs. The eggs were hard-shelled and about an eighth of an inch in diameter. They were hatching, and the young were stuck together with a gelatinous substance which covered them. Waterton (see Eigenmann and Allen, 1942, p. 245) says piranhas spawn on liana roots in the water.

Hartt (1870, p. 401) gives a very circumstantial account of the breeding, as told to him by fishermen on the S. Francisco River. The fish clean out a shallow nest on the sandy bottom and spawn in it. The female guards the nest and viciously attacks any animal or human who comes near. The laying

An adult "silver dollar" pacu of the genus *Mylossoma*. Compare the very short adipose fin with the long, low adipose of *Metynnis*. Photo by Dr. Herbert R. Axelrod.

Young of one of the "silver dollar" pacu of the genus *Metynnis*. Photo by Dr. Herbert R. Axelrod.

is said to take place principally in October soon after the rains raise the water level. Almost certainly the species was *S. piraya*.

Few fishes of the family Characidae make nests or guard the young, but Hartt's account seems so straightforward that I am inclined to believe it, even though it is second-hand. The characin *Copeina* has much stranger breeding habits and the *Erythrinus*-like forms are said to guard the eggs. I have seen the nest and the guarding parent of *Hoplias* myself, and the nest is much as Hartt describes for the piranha.

Perhaps Brown and Waterton were right about the Guiana species, but I refuse to believe, without better evidence, that in one species of piranha both parents guard the nest and in another only one. But surely no other fish is so well prepared to protect its young as a piranha! And the consensus seems to be that they do guard the eggs and young.

[Supplementary note, 1971.—Piranhas have now bred a few times in captivity, the ones I have heard about having occurred in large tanks in public aquaria. They guard the eggs.—G.S.M.]

The piranha is chiefly a fish-eater but not infrequently terrestrial animals become its prey. Hartley mentions that the kiskadees in Guiana occasionally fly down to pick up an insect floating on the water. Then, as he says, "there is a flash of wings, a slight splash, and the bird returns to its perch clicking its bill and swallowing contentedly. The splash is often its undoing, for, at the sound, a dark body moves swiftly through the water and the kiskadee is dragged under with its prey still struggling in its beak." Several observations are on record of reptile-eating birds flying low over the water, trailing their prey from their talons, and having the reptile snatched from them by piranhas. Almost any animal which falls into the water accidentally is likely to be set upon and eaten, like the unfortunate boy mentioned by Hartt, who fell off a pier when frightened by a cannon shot and was immediately devoured.

Probably piranhas feed normally on any fish they can catch, chiefly the smaller kinds. Magalhaes (1931, p. 167), who observed piranhas in the Amazon, says that they do not hesitate to attack any fish, however large, if they are hungry. I cannot believe that they do this habitually, or none of the great fishes of that river would ever reach maturity, but I do believe that they will immediately attack even the river porpoises and the giant catfishes if these creatures happen to be wounded or are behaving in an unnatural manner. Among most predaceous fishes, including sharks, such unnatural behavior or thrashing about always invites attack. Other large fish, or human beings, which move quietly or remain quite still are seldom molested.

Many writers refer to the piranhas eating vegetable matter at times. They can be caught on hooks baited by dough balls. They are also known to eat fruit. It would be strange if fishes so closely related to the pacús did not

46

occasionally do so. The reverse, however, does not appear to occur. No species of pacú has teeth fitted to cut flesh, and although I suspect that they might bite people, as other characins do, nobody has ever reported being bitten by them.

WHY PIRANHAS BEHAVE AS THEY DO

Almost everyone who has written on piranhas has marvelled at several features of their habits—their sensitivity to the taint of blood in the water, the nervous dash with which they attack moving objects, and especially the fact that kicking or splashing *attracts* them in hordes instead of driving them away. To my knowledge, no one has ever attempted to explain these things, in spite of the fact that the reasons for them are obvious.

In regard to smelling blood in the water, it can be said that nearly all fishes seem to be able to "smell" very well anything like blood that is dissolved in the water. This is not at all remarkable. But the other things are, and they relate directly to habits of the characins as a group, some of which habits can be observed in the small characins we keep in home aquaria.

A certain group of the characins, including many of our small aquarium species, are very nervous fishes. This group is what might be called the "silvery characins" as opposed to the "dark-colored characins" such as *Hoplias, Chilodus, Leporinus, Prochilodus, Curimata*, etc. The "silvery" ones include *Charax*, the pacus, the piranhas, and most of the small species we call tetras *(Tetragonopterus* and its allies). These are nervous fishes. We can see that the little ones in an aquarium keep up a constant "flicking" of the pectoral fins, and they tend to dash off, after food at the surface, or away in fright, far more quickly than most other small fresh-water fishes.

The habit of being attracted by a commotion in the water has to be studied in larger space than an aquarium will allow, but it is a very deep-seated trait of all the "silvery" characins. Breder (1927) and I (Myers, 1932) have already published the essential facts in regard to this habit in small characins of the genus *Astyanax*, in Panama and Texas. At Phantom Lake in west Texas, I lay down in the warm clear water at the shore. The splashing of my entrance frightened the minnows away but attracted hordes of this small characin. The 3- and 4-inch fish clustered about me, alert to any movement I made. If I suddenly wriggled a toe, the whole crowd of fish (it was scarcely what I could call a school) would flash down to my foot, and surround it with an eager mass of little silvery fishes—all keeping a foot or more away, but alert, relatively motionless and waiting. Movement of a finger caused a lightning-like shift of fish and interest, but they never came close enough to bite.

Breder, in Panama, found the slightly larger *Astyanax ruberrimus* to be less backward. Although under 6 inches long, these little fellows were not only attracted by Dr. Breder, but they actually closed in on him and bit, and their

A *Metynnis* species. Photo by Dr. Herbert R. Axelrod.

A species of pacu of the genus *Myloplus*. Photo by Dr. Herbert R. Axelrod.

attacks upon the tenderer portions of his anatomy while swimming (as he told me personally) were scarcely describable as painless.

Later, I had a similar experience with an even smaller characin, in Lagoa Santa, in Brazil. We swam in the warm water off the dock and were immediately surrounded by thousands of an elongate, pale, silvery species of *Hemigrammus* under 2 inches long. These occurred in vast shoals in the very clear water of the lake and evidently formed the food of the *Serrasalmus* (pirambeba) found there. Although strong swimming and kicking kept them off, it attracted them in swarms, and the moment a swimmer slowed down they closed in to attack. They were too tiny to bite one's skin but they seized upon every hair and jerked for dear life! Several hundred of them tugging and snapping at once became exceedingly annoying.

Evidently the more dangerous piranhas act exactly like the much smaller characins which attacked Breder and me. Splashing and quick movements attract them, and since they probably have no other aquatic creature whatsoever to fear, they have no reason not to be bold. When, in addition to the attraction of splashing and kicking, they smell blood, any fear they may have had is overcome, and they flash in and snap just as their smaller relatives may be seen to do in an aquarium when fed on chopped raw meat.

LITERATURE CITED

Barnhart, Clarence L. (editor). 1947. "The American College Dictionary." New York.

Breder, Charles M. 1927. "The Fishes of the Rio Chucunaque Drainage, Eastern Panama." In: Bulletin of the American Museum of Natural History, vol. 57, art. 3. New York.

Brehm, Alfred. 1920. "Die Fische." In: Brehms Tierleben, zweiter Neudruck der vierten Auflage. Leipzig und Wien.

Burton, Richard F. 1869. "The Highlands of the Brazil." 2 vols. London.

Castelnau, Francis de. 1855. "Animaux nouveaux ou rares . . . . Amerique du Sud." Poissons. Paris.

Cutright, Paul Russell. 1940. "The Great Naturalists Explore South America." New York.

Devincenzi, G. J. and Teague, G. W. 1942. "Ictiofauna del Rio Uruguay Medio." In: Anales del Museo de Historia Natural de Montevideo, ser. 2, toma 5, no. 4. Montevideo, Uruguay.

Eigenmann, Carl H. 1915. "The Serrasalminae and Mylinae." In: Annals of the Carnegie Museum, vol. 9, nos. 3 and 4. Pittsburgh, Pa.

Eigenmann, C. H. and Allen, Wm. R. 1942. "Fishes of Western South America." Lexington, Kentucky.

Gill, Theo. N. 1907. "Parental Care Among Fresh Water Fishes." In: Annual Report of the Smithsonian Institution for 1905. Washington, D.C.

Hartley, G. Inness. 1917. "Notes on the Perai Fish." In: Beebe, Hartley, and Howes, "Tropical Wild Life in British Guiana." New York.

Hartt, Charles Frederick. 1870. "Geology and Physical Geography of Brazil." In: Thayer Expedition: Scientific Results of a Journey in Brazil, by Louis Agassiz and his travelling companions. Boston.

Holder, C. F. 1883. "The Nest-Builders of the Sea." In: Harper's New Monthly Magazine, for December, 1883, vol. 68.

Humboldt, A. von, and Valenciennes, A. 1817. "Recherches sur les Poissons Fluviatiles de l'Amerique Equinoxiale." In: Humboldt and Bonpland, Recueil d'observations de Zoologie, etc.

Ihering, Rodolpho von. 1934. "Da Vida dos Nossos Animais: Fauna do Brasil." São Leopoldo, Rio Grande do Sul.

Ihering, Rodolpho von. 1940. "Dicionario dos Animais do Brasil." São Paulo.

Luetken, Christian F. 1875. "Velhas-Flodens Fiske." In: Memoires de l'Academie Royale de Copenhague, ser. 5, vol. 12, no. 2. Copenhagen.

Magalhaes, Agenor Couto de. 1931. "Monographia Brazileira de Peixes Fluviaes." Sao Paulo.

Marcgrave, George. 1648. "Historia Naturalis Brasiliae." Leiden and Amsterdam.

Myers, George S. 1932. "Some Notes on the Characin, Astyanax mexicanus, in Texas." In: Aquatic Life, vol. 16, no. 3. Baltimore.

Norman, John R. 1929. "The South American Characid Fishes of the Subfamily Serrasalmoninae, with a Revision of the Genus Serrasalmus." In: Proceedings of the Zoological Society of London for 1928. London.

Pinto, Alfredo Moreira. 1899. "Apontamentos para o Diccionario Geographico do Brazil." 3 vols. Rio de Janeiro, 1894–99.

Rondon, Candido Mariano da Silva. n.d. "Relatorio, vol. 1, Estudos e Reconhecimentos." In: Commissão de Linhas Telegraphicas Estrategicas de Matto Grosso ao Amazonas, publicacão no. 1. Rio de Janeiro. (Published about 1910.)

Roosevelt, Theodore. 1914. "Through the Brazilian Wilderness." New York. (Also later reprints.)

Roth, Vincent. 1943. "Notes and Observations on Fish Life in British Guiana, a Popular Guide to Colonial Fishes." In: The Guiana Edition, no. 8. Georgetown, British Guiana.

Schomburgk, Robert Hermann. 1843. "Fishes of British Guiana." 2 vols. In: The Naturalist's Library, edited by Sir Wm. Jardine, vols. 30 and 31. London.

Sousa, Gabriel Soares de. (1825.) "Tratado Descriptivo do Brasil em 1587." Terceira Edicão. In: Brasiliana, vol. 117. São Paulo, 1938. (Originally printed in 1825.)

Stradelli, E. 1929. "Vocabularios da Lingua Geral . . . ." In: Revista do Instituto Historico e Geographico Brasileiro, tomo 104, vol. 158. Rio de Janeiro.

Up de Graf, F. W. 1923. "Head Hunters of the Amazon." Garden City, New York.

Verissimo, Jose. 1895. "A Pesca na Amazonia." Rio de Janeiro and São Paulo.

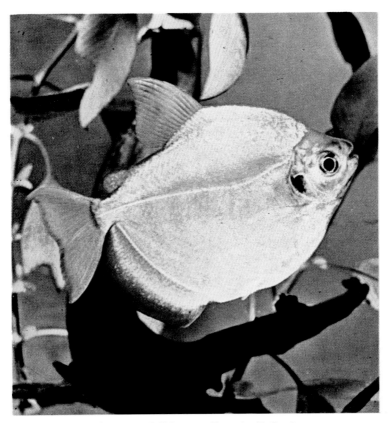

A species of *Mylossoma*. Photo by H. Franke.

Metynnis species. Photo by Kremser.

* Appeared in the August, 1965 issue of *Tropical Fish Hobbyist*.

Species of Piranhas*

BY DR. GEORGE S. MYERS

Almost everybody these days knows about the South American characid fishes called *piranha* (pronounced *peer-on-yah*) in Brazil and *caribe* (*kah-reé-bay*) in Venezuela. Some of them are very dangerous to man, and many fishermen who live where these fishes abound have lost fingers or toes—if not their lives—to voracious piranhas. However, that is not what I wish to talk about here.

Ichthyologists know that there are a number of kinds, or species, of *Serrasalmus*, the generic name under which the piranhas are classified. For one thing, fishermen on many of the Brazilian rivers recognize two general types of piranhas—the snub-nosed, compact *piranhas verdadeiras* or true piranhas (pronounced *vair-dah-day-ras*) which are highly dangerous, and the less snub-nosed, somewhat more elongated kinds of *pirambebas* (pronounced *peer-om-bay-bas*). Pirambeba-type *Serrasalmus* are rarely dangerous to human beings, although they can cause havoc amongst other fishes of their own size or smaller.

In fact, ichthyologists used to classify piranhas under two or three different generic names—*Serrasalmus* (or *Serrasalmo*) for the pirambeba-type fishes, and *Pygocentrus*, *Rooseveltiella* (for Teddy Roosevelt) or *Taddyella* (also for Teddy!) for the snub-nosed, more dangerous forms. However, this multiple generic arrangement was dropped nearly 40 years ago, and all piranha-like fishes save one *(Pygopristis denticulatus)* are now placed in the single genus *Serrasalmus*. Only incorrigible "splitters" have a different opinion.

When we come to the species, ichthyologists have assumed that the piranhas were pretty well classified, following earlier work by the late Dr. Eigenmann and the revisional study made by an eminent ichthyologist, the late J. R. Norman of the British Museum, and published in the Proceedings of the Zoological Society of London in 1929. That study was based on what seemed at the time to be large and reasonably adequate samples of preserved piranha specimens in the British Museum. However, man-made classifications of any creatures have a disconcerting way of "coming unstuck" when much larger collections of study-specimens become available. Plants and animals vary, from place to place, and characteristics which appear to separate two species in one locality often do not do so in others (from which specimens did not happen to be available for previous research).

For reasons of this type—and others—the classification of the species of *Serrasalmus* has "come unstuck" in a big way, although very little hint of this is so far to be found in the literature of ichthyology. A number of years ago, during the examination of piranha specimens from Venezuela (a very large area from which neither Eigenmann nor Norman had adequate specimen-samples), I found that a number of specimens were hard to place.

More recently, a colleague and former pupil of mine, Dr. Alan E. Leviton, began an examination of a collection of piranha specimens far larger (for some areas) than those Eigenmann or Norman used. Although he had to drop the study temporarily, he did find that the situation in regard to classification of piranha species is much worse than I had imagined. Not only did some of the supposedly best-known species appear to merge (once specimens from certain places were examined) but even the distinction between pirambeba-type and piranha-type does not always seem to be well marked.

In any event, once Dr. Leviton had shown me some of his material, he convinced me that putting a scientific name on any but two or three very distinctive species is a very risky business at the present time. What is obviously necessary to a proper understanding of piranha classification is a study vastly more extensive than any yet made. And it seems highly possible that all the thousands of specimens of piranhas now preserved in museum collections are insufficient for such a study.

Mylossoma species. Photo by Dr. Herbert R. Axelrod.

An unidentified species of pacu. Photo by Dr. Herbert R. Axelrod.

A young *Myloplus* pacu. Photo by Dr. Herbert R. Axelrod.

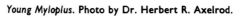
Young Myloplus. Photo by Dr. Herbert R. Axelrod.

Supplementary Notes on the Classification of Piranhas

By George S. Myers

My short reprinted article on the classification of the piranhas, which is reproduced in this book, is now several years old, and some new information is given here.

The classification of piranha species is still in confusion. Although Dr. Leviton, mentioned in the article referred to, has been unable to continue his work on the piranhas, other work on this subject has been or is being done. For example, Messrs. Ramirez and Fernandez-Yepez of Venezuela have described and named a number of presumed new species from Venezuela, some jointly with each other, some by each author separately. I have no idea whether some or all of these supposedly different species are really valid, although I am inclined to suspect that at least some of them are not, simply because neither Mr. Fernandez-Yepez nor Mr. Ramirez has made the kind of painstaking laboratory study of thousands of specimens that must be a part of any solution of the problem. There are no short-cuts!

Dr. Jacques Gery, the French specialist on characoid fishes, has also been working on the piranhas and believes that *Serrasalmus* and its close relatives should be placed in a separate family, Serrasalmidae. Mr. Fernandez-Yepez and possibly some others have accepted this change, but the principal authority on the anatomy and classification of the characoids, Dr. Stanley H. Weitzman of the Smithsonian Institution, does not, and I agree fully with him in this regard.

Certain recent writers on characoid fishes have revived usage of the generic name *Pygocentrus* for the most dangerous of the piranhas, or use the generic names *Rooseveltiella* or *Taddyella*. I do not believe that it serves any useful purpose whatsoever to split off the more dangerous species as a different genus or different genera. In any event, there has been some recent misuse of the name *Rooseveltiella*, and this misuse should be explained. *Pygocentrus* was originally proposed solely for *Serrasalmus piraya*, the large dangerous species of the Rio São Francisco, which remains the nomenclatural type of the generic name *Pygocentrus*. (Do not confuse this name with *Pygopristis*.) The limits of *Pygocentrus* were later enlarged to include all the dangerous snub-nosed species, including the black piranha, *S. niger*. Much later, Eigenmann restricted *Pygocentrus* again to *S. piraya* and proposed *Rooseveltiella* for *S. nattereri* and its close relatives. This name was given in honor of President Theodore Roosevelt. Unknown to Eigenmann, however, the generic name *Rooseveltiella* had previously been used for some other animal genus and so cannot be used for this fish. It was then replaced by *Taddyella*, the proposer of which thought he was also naming it for "Teddy" Roosevelt, but got the spelling wrong. The result is that the dangerous piranhas may (1) be left in *Serrasalmus*, where I think they belong or (2) be split off as the separate genus *Pygocentrus* or (3) be split off as two separate genera *(Pygocentrus* and *Taddyella)*. This last solution, in my opinion, is certainly going too far.

However, while species are usually definable, objective entities, genera always have been and always will be highly subjective entities, subject to the judgment and opinion of taxonomists, some of whom tend to lump and some to split genera. I try to follow a middle course, but in this particular case I think lumping is in order.

While on this subject of names, it should be mentioned that some recent South American writers on ichthyology, notably Drs. Ringuelet and Aramburu in Argentina, have discontinued the use of the well known familial name Characidae and now use in place of it the name Tetragonopteridae. The rules for the nomenclature of families and other categories in zoology are laid down in the International Code of Zoological Nomenclature. In regard to families, however, the determining procedure is rather complicated and requires a really exhaustive search of usages in the older literature. I have recently made such a search and have carefully studied the governing provisions of the Code. While there are some complicating factors which I shall not go into at this time, my conclusions are that the name Characidae is valid for the family because it is the oldest, whereas the family-group name Tetragonopteridae (or variations of it) are all younger, and that name must give way to the better-known name Characidae.

Finally, Dr. James E. Boehlke, of the Academy of Natural Sciences of Philadelphia, has taken up a long-term study of piranhas, based on large series of specimens and extensive field work within a restricted area, in an attempt to determine the limits of variability within single species in that area. It is hoped that his studies will tell us much about piranha species that other types of work have not so far produced.

One of the difficulties of properly delimiting piranha (and other fish) species in the great rivers of South America is the fact that great changes in these rivers occurred in relatively recent geological time, thus in effect scrambling fish distribution in a most effective way. In the year 1960 (in the scientific journal *Evolution*) I published papers on the evolution of fishes in

Myloplus schomburgki. Photo by Dr. Herbert R. Axelrod.

Young of a species of *Mylossoma*. Photo by Dr. Herbert R. Axelrod.

A *Myloplus* species. Photo by Dr. Herbert R. Axelrod.

great lakes (especially Lake Lanao, Tanganyika, Nyasa or Malawi, etc.) in which I attempted some explanation for rich fish faunas of these lakes today. In some cases such evolution has taken place to a remarkable degree in such a short geological time as 10,000 years. At the same time I also pointed out that the great but fluctuating lakes along the lower Amazon also provide probably similar conditions, in which rapid fish evolution could occur. However, this is not the only factor. During the last million or two years (Pleistocene or Quaternary time), the great Ice Age piled up astonishingly great amounts of ice on the northernmost and southernmost land areas, thus greatly lowering sea level around the globe. But during this time there were colder glacial periods (more ice, lower seas) and warmer interglacial periods (little ice, much higher seas). We are now in an intermediate stage (considerable ice, intermediate sea level). During the Quaternary, sea level has at times been much lower and at others much higher than at present. Some geologists think that the sea was as much as 300 feet higher than at present during warmer interglacial periods and at least that much lower during glacials.

It is easy to imagine what these changes in sea level would do to the lowlands of our great river basins. When the level went down, the great lowlands would be drained and the rivers would run in deep trenches or canyons. (This has been carefully worked out by geologists for the lower Mississippi Valley.) When sea level went up, the lowlands would be deeply flooded, forming great lakes which would last for the ten to fifty or more thousand years that level was high. Whether the flooding was of fresh or salt water would depend on rainfall (which also varied) and on whether the river lowlands showed physical features (chains of hills, etc.) to hold out the sea to some extent.

The lower Amazon has a chain of such hills which run south to the main river at Monte Alegre and another which runs north to near the river from south of that point. These hills form a sort of bottleneck on the lower Amazon at Monte Alegre—a bottle-neck which may have prevented much incursion of salt water above that point during sea level higher than at present. It seems certain that during some periods of the Quaternary the lower Amazon basin was a great lake, perhaps salt, perhaps fresh, and perhaps with heavier salt water underlying the lighter fresh water. If the sea stood 150 feet above present level, the flooding would have extended west almost to the present border of Peru, and this is a reasonable estimate.

The scrambling of freshwater fish populations that would have occurred during these 10-, 20-, 50- or 100 thousand year intervals is obvious. And the last great change (at the time of the Wisconsin Glaciation) was only yesterday, in the geological and evolutionary sense. During each time of high and each time of low water there was plenty of time for the evolution of large numbers of fish species adapted to conditions at the time. With slow change from high to low, or the reverse, many species would be wiped out, but some would survive or adapt to the new conditions, to be added to all those which had lasted in the same way from the previous changes.

The lowlands of the lower Amazon themselves seem to have been more free of tectonic changes (changes in level of the land itself due to geophysical causes) than most land areas of similar extent throughout the world. The great ancient rock masses (cratons) or Guyana (to the north) and Brazil (to the south) probably were restive during the Quaternary, as they were before, but this probably had comparatively little effect on the great lowlands of silt along the river, leaving changes of sea level as the principal causes of changed conditions affecting the fishes. For a long time, geologists have postulated a lakelike flooded Amazon basin during most of the time since the first major rise of the Andes Mountains at the beginning of Tertiary time. Was this a partially or wholly sea-flooded basin, or was it largely of fresh water? Was it caused by tectonic movement of the land itself? I doubt it. It seems much more likely that it was caused by a world-wide sea level which, before the beginning of Quaternary glaciation, must have been considerably higher than at present for many millions of years.

In any event, it can easily be seen how geological events must have seriously affected fish distribution and evolution—some of it during relatively recent time.

No wonder piranha classification is difficult!

Cambridge, Mass.—November 1971.

Catoprion mento, the only species of the pacu group having a strongly projecting lower jaw. The species' principal food consists of scales scraped off other living fishes by means of its wide-set sharp teeth. Photo by Dr. Herbert R. Axelrod.

The relatively harmless pacu species such as *Metynnis* and *Mylossoma* usually are maintained in bare aquaria or in aquaria that contain either plastic plants or living plants that are unreachable by the fishes, as the *Metynnis* and *Mylossoma* species eat plants readily; the dangerous piranhas do not. This is a dangerous piranha species. Photo by Dr. Herbert R. Axelrod.

Piranhas—Fact and Fiction

HARALD SCHULTZ,
Museu Paulista,
São Paulo, Brazil.
Photos by the author

"When my father was fifteen years old, he fled from attacking Indians in a little, wobbly dugout canoe. The boat tipped over, and he escaped by swimming, but when he climbed out of the water he was a skeleton! Later nothing like that could ever happen to him again! . . ."

Similar and just as absurd stories may be read in many books about the Amazon. And the worst of it is that the authors are taken seriously.

To my astonishment I have even found horror stories about Piranhas in serious scientific notes. There is even talk that many of the male natives in the Brazilian part of the Paraguay river region have been attacked while swimming nude.

For more than twenty years my travels as a student of Indian life in connection with a scientific institute in Brazil have taken me to many far distant parts of the country. In all these years I have never had a harmful experience with these greatly feared Piranhas.

It is not necessary to go as far as the Amazon to see Piranhas. They are native to all the larger river systems of Brazil, with the exception of the smaller streams in the southern part of the country which do not connect

The author used to tie all sorts of things to his feet and legs before he stepped into the Amazon to look for new fish species. But after a time this procedure was a nuisance. Now he does not do this any more, but wades into all shallow waters up to the navel and deeper, wearing only bathing trunks or long trousers which have been rolled up, whichever is handiest. Only once was he bitten on the big toe by a Piranha, when he left a netful of *wounded* fish on the shore and waded back into the water. The Piranhas were attracted by the dead and dying fish which are always damaged when a net is drawn, and one bit his big toe, without successfully removing a chunk of flesh.

with the La Plata, São Francisco or the Amazon. Probably the climate in these subtropic waters is not proper for these warmth-requiring fishes, but there may be other reasons for their absence.

The most vicious and dangerous Piranhas are supposed to occur in the Rio São Francisco, the only river which originates in Brazil and empties into the ocean. In 1938 I sailed down the São Francisco in a slow paddlewheel steamer. The ship grounded several times and the deck-hands had to go overboard to get it afloat. None of them even considered the possibility of any danger from Piranhas. They remained in the water for almost an hour, scantily clad, standing, wading and pushing until we were again afloat.

The Piranhas of the Paraguay, which belongs to the La Plata System, are supposed to be "very bad". I spent eight months on its shores with the little-known Umutina Indians. We amused ourselves almost daily by swimming in the river. There were plenty of Piranhas! The Indians had no fear of them, but they spoke repeatedly in frightened voices and gestures of one thing: **Shuré**! I continued to bathe happily until I realized that they meant the giant snake, the Anaconda, which is Brazil's largest. They told me, and I have heard other reliable accounts, that they could seize a grown person and drag him under the water, naturally drowning him. It would be a lie, however, to say that they could afterwards swallow such a huge morsel as an adult human body!

The natives spent many hours in the water when they fished by poisoning the water with timbó vines, but never was there one injured by Piranhas.

In most rivers where there are Piranhas one can see crowds of naked and almost naked children and adults romping and playing among schools of the fearsome Piranhas. On the Mortes, the River of Death, the native laundresses sit in the crystal-clear water with half of their naked bodies in the water. Among them swim the beautiful red-and-gold, the white, and the huge black Piranhas. Still, nothing ever happens to these ladies!

Naturally, the natives of the Brazilian jungles know where and when they can swim, and avoid swimming unnecessarily far out in Piranha-infested waters. Here one bathes in the shallow parts, and avoids making a lot of noise. Accidents with Piranhas happen exactly as do traffic accidents in civilized sections, but not nearly as often.

The Black Piranha (pronounced pih-rán-ya) is a fast swimmer. Its muscular body lets it inhabit deeper waters. They are found in places where the strong current causes the waters to be shunned by smaller fishes. This fish was caught in a few seconds in a spot where the Rio Japurá natives swam daily. And there must doubtless have been many more Black Piranhas nearby. Never was a bather molested by them.

The head of almost all Piranha species is armored with strong bony plates, sometimes a very strong pair of gill-plates. Strong muscles, which are well developed in the "dangerous" species, give the underjaw great strength. The head of the species which are dangerous to man is short, compressed, and looks a little like a bulldog. Once the sharp teeth have grasped their prey they do not let go easily, until it has been bitten to pieces. The razor-sharp teeth of the Piranha are normally only partly visible, because they are covered by the fleshy lips. In order to see them better, the lips have been cut away from this (dead) specimen. Piranhas have only a single row of pyramid-like teeth. The points of the teeth in the upper jaw fit exactly into the grooves of the lower row, making them capable of inflicting a smooth bite which bleeds copiously and is very painful. If the fish cannot free the chunk he has bitten, he turns his head in a semicircle until the bite is free.

In the two decades of my travels in the jungle, I have met seven persons (of all the many thousands with whom I came in contact!) who have been injured by Piranhas. These were all slight bites. I heard about a boy who capsized in the middle of the stream and was eaten by Piranhas. His ghost is supposed to have remained behind, and some who were acquainted with this story assumed that the boy might have drowned and that the Piranhas ate him afterwards.

Once when I was spearing the big Pirarucú (*Arapaima gigas*) with the Karajá Indians I heard a loud outcry from the shore. A hunter had wounded a water-hog. With its last strength it leaped into the water. The hunter wanted to retrieve his kill and stepped into the water to pull it out. The bleeding animal had attracted a school of red Piranhas (*Serrasalmus nattereri*). One bit the hunter in the thigh. The wound was flat and smooth, as if made with a sharp knife, bled freely and seemed very painful. The man, however, was able to climb by his own power out of the dangerous waters.

The head of the Red Piranha is very short and compressed, and it can be seen that it could belong to the species most dangerous to man. The underjaw is powered by a very strong head musculature and enables it to take small, flat bites out of its prey. The Red Piranha is rightfully one of the most feared in the entire Amazon Basin, and at the same time one of the most widely distributed. It attains a maximum length of 8 inches, and is considered one of the "smaller" species. These gold and red predators swim with lightning speed to tear one of their own number to pieces if it is injured when removing the hook and returned to the water.

Not always is it necessary to have blood in the water to attract schools of Piranhas. These Brazilian waters are endlessly big, and every cubic yard of water does not necessarily contain a Piranha! As far as I could find out, they travel in schools which are self-regulated in large territories, which would eliminate their being found as single individuals. Piranhas are excellent, fast swimmers. If anything out of the ordinary takes place the entire, always-growing swarm is shortly congregated there. Injured Piranhas or those with scars of battle are never found in nature. We can only speak of them as "school fish" in a limited manner. A horde of Piranhas guards its own territory, but the individuals do not stay together in any regular formation. They also do not permit many other fishes in their territory. For this reason it is a well-known fact that wherever Piranhas are caught, it is seldom that any other fish are hooked. The greedy Piranhas see to that!

In Rio Sinho, a little tributary stream of the Javahé in central Brazil, well known for its great numbers of the feared red-and-gold species, I shot a water-hog for our midday meal. The shot was a good one. The animal in its death throes leaped from the bank and into the water. Here the current was strong. I figured the meal was lost. Not so our native guide. After a great deal of work he found it with a long pole. It lay in about five feet of water, pressed down into the sand by its own weight. The Javahé Indian dived down, and we were able to drag the 100-pound animal into the dugout. It was completely undamaged, in spite of attracting Piranhas and other fishes.

Toward noon, when we had found a shady spot to cook our meal, I cut off a piece of the meat and washed it in very shallow water, about 8 inches deep. Everywhere there were big schools of thousands of little silvery Tetras which gobbled up anything edible they could find . . . they even nibbled at the bathers. Then unexpectedly there came some half-grown red-and-gold Piranhas from the deeper waters of the slow-flowing stream. These are the most beautiful Piranhas I know of. Seldom are these highly-colored fish seen

The head of *Pygopristis denticulatus* is scarcely set off from the body and only a slight, almost invisible dent indicates where the head really begins. The blunt mouth contains sharp rows of teeth, although they are concealed by thick lips. Powerful musculature enables them to make successful attacks on all sorts of animal life, primarily the sick, old or dead of their own species. Exact examination of the stomach contents of freshly caught specimens could give more exact information.

Serrasalmus spilopleura perhaps marks a transition to the "less dangerous" species, although every Piranha must be treated with respect if for instance a bather with bloody wounds finds himself in water where these fish are numerous. With *spilopleura* the head sets away from the rest of the body, but the strong mouth with the thick lips betrays the sharp teeth which are hidden beneath and can be dangerously wielded by the powerful lower jaw muscles. The lower body of this species, which is easily seen in the foregoing picture, is almost knife-edged, narrow, less rounded than with most Piranha species. The face is not as blank, almost "stupid," as for example that of the Red Piranha.

Serrasalmus nattereri, the Red Piranha, is doubtless one of the most beautiful and feared of all the Piranha species. Head and back are brownish to olive, face and upper half of the back gold to silvery. From the mouth back there is diffused over the entire body as far as the anal fin (inclusive) a gleaming red. The tail is almost black, with a lighter stripe in the middle. It is not only one of the most beautiful Piranha species, but one of the most colorful of all the freshwater fishes that I know. There seem to be several color varieties of this species. The prettiest come from the Araguaia river, where they are very numerous.

in our show-tanks. They threw themselves at the chunk of meat and bit into it so hard that I was able to lift bunches of them out of the water before they would let go. We let them drop into a clean, water-filled gasoline can. Unfortunately they did not last long, even when we kept only one in a can. As long as they had such a bloodthirsty appetite, none of us naturally had the desire to bathe. Shortly thereafter I had to go into the water! One of my shoes fell into the water and sank. I went fully dressed into the stream and dived. My hands and part of my arms were exposed. The Piranhas did not bother with me!

The method described above is the best way to catch Piranhas. If they are caught in a seine, they soon ruin it. Even the first drag of the net will result in many escaping through holes which they have bitten. If caught on a hook, they usually die from the injury sustained.

One account having to do with Piranhas has become famous in Brazil.

Some Indians and many natives are in the habit of standing in the water while fishing. Lacking better equipment, fish which are caught are killed by biting them just behind the head. Often the fish is held in the teeth until the hook is again baited, and then it is thrown on the shore. Illogical? Maybe, but that's how it's done.

A soldier of the eminent and world-famous Brazilian Indian General Candido y Mariano da Silva Rondon (who died as Marshal in 1959), one of the greatest authorities in the world on jungle life, fished in his free time from an island in the river. He caught a Piranha and killed it with the traditional bite behind the head, which is usually reserved for the more harmless species. He held it firmly with his teeth . . . and the beast retaliated by biting off part of his tongue! By the time help arrived in answer to his frightful, choking cries he had almost bled to death!

Piranhas scarcely ever attack uninjured animals or humans. Some years ago we found a little pond, crystal-clear, in one of the sandbanks. It was river water, left behind by the receding waters after the rainy season. The Indians had taken us there, so that we could collect fishes with our net of thin nylon mesh. Large Cichlids of the genus *Geophagus*, wonderfully colored, with long dorsal filaments swam in schools and soon became entangled in the hair-thin meshes of our available net. As they struggled medium-sized Piranhas,

Happy Indian children play in the Amazon waters, where there are Piranhas. Where is the often mentioned danger?

On the Island of Marajo, the largest island in the Amazon Delta, as large as Switzerland, there are many lakes which dry out in the summer. Countless fishes, among them thousands of the "dangerous" Red Piranhas, are squeezed together in close quarters. Fishermen come from Belem do Pará and other regions to get these "riches" from the lakes before they dry out completely. Long cotton seines are stretched out and pulled to the shore by the fishermen, who are sometimes in water up to their necks. They wear only trousers to give some protection to their bodies, but feet, legs and upper bodies are bare. Also here there is no thought of any possible danger from Piranhas. But every Amazon native has great fear of the Stingrays which lie on the bottom of these waters.

Serrasalmus spilopleura, attacked the helpless Cichlids and ate them from the tail on, until only the heads were hanging from the net!

If bathers are uninjured, they will scarcely ever be attacked. However, if one has a wound, there is always the possibility that Piranhas could be attracted and go into an attack. If one finds himself injured and far from the shore, say about 10 or 15 yards, there is a possibility that the shore could not be reached without help, and that he would find himself a prey to the Piranhas. Piranhas like to rush about in slowly-flowing waters near the shore. Their bites are painful and the loss of blood great. It is only too understandable that the soft portions of their prey will be attacked first.

Once they have attacked, these beasts will allow nothing to drive them off. On the contrary, the more the victim thrashes about, the more Piranhas will be attracted. It is an established method when fishing for them to beat the water with the fishing-rod and thereby to attract these fish.

Where there are many Piranhas, it is possible to observe how the big fish will sometimes seek shelter in shallow water. They are occasionally seen lying with half the body out of water. These are always fish which have become wounded or are sick, weak or old, who by their unnatural behavior have attracted the attention of the Piranhas and drawn them there. Healthy fish, in my experience, are eaten only in the rarest instances.

One would be led to believe that in waters which are "infested" with Piranhas there would be countless big fish which have reached a considerable age. However, there are hundreds of thousands of crocodiles, a great many turtles, river dolphins and giant otters which swim with their babies in beautiful formations in the water, all of which certainly eat Piranhas. Water-hogs live in great herds on the shores and when attacked dive into deep water, as do the little paccas and large tapirs which lie lazily in the water during the hot hours of the day. What would happen to these animals, if they were regularly attacked and eaten by Piranhas? And what would the Piranhas eat, once all the animals were eaten? Today much of the great, lovely animal world of Brazil has disappeared, having fallen a prey to the bullets of inconsiderate hunters. But there are just as many Piranhas as there were then, still untouched by the life of the jungle.

I consider Piranhas as excellent aquarium fishes! They are not for the hobbyist with small aquaria, but for large show-tanks. It is only a problem of space to keep Piranhas, so that they will not injure each other; individually they can also be kept in smaller aquaria.

Pygopristis denticulatus (Cuvier) differs from the previous species by a less sharply offset head, the black edging of the caudal and anal fins and the almost silvery unflecked body. Pectoral and ventral fins are a beautiful gleaming chrome yellow, which is not the case with most other species. Nobody fears this Piranha when bathing, as is the case with most of the others. We purposely show here a Piranha which by the form of its head again signifies "a step back" to the more dangerous species. This fish in the illustration was caught by the author in the Upper Guaporé.

Serrasalmus hollandi, from the Upper Guaporé like the previous species, is called *Piranha saicanga* by the Brazilian natives. This fish is elongated, almost elliptical. The head is long, the lower body edge sharp, the ventral fins pointed and tinted a pretty red and the tail almost transparent with a black caudal base. The body is silvery, with a few dark patches in rows. It is one of the smaller species which attains a length of about 6 inches.

Piranhas are genuine Characins, or Tetras, and as such possess the typical adipose fin. Some of the most beautiful fishes which I know of in our hobby certainly belong to this group. *Serrasalmus nattereri*, which is plentiful in many of the rivers which comprise the Amazon, has a lovely coloration.

According to Myers[1] there are about 16 Piranha species, of which only four could be considered dangerous to humans. In Brazil they are known collectively as Piranhas. But the natives of the interior distinguish the various species by their colors: white, red, spotted and black Piranhas. The other native names, such as *Piranha-saicanga* or even *Piranha-caju* are suggested by their appearance. *Caju* is a well-known Brazilian fruit whose outer kernel is roasted and eaten by us. A species which is not placed in the ranks of the Piranhas by the ichthyologists is the *Catoprion mento*, known as the Wimple Piranha.

I have observed an intentional order in the illustration to show the transition from the "genuine", that is the more dangerously equipped and inclined species, to those with weaker jaw muscles which usually have bigger mouths.

The fact that Piranhas injure each other is, as has been stated already, mainly a question of space. When a Piranha is caught it snaps at anything that gets in the way of its extremely sharp jaws, and does not let go! A newly-caught, excited Piranha would automatically bite at its own kind if it got near, therefore the advice against too close quarters.

I once had to ship a Piranha which had been kept in captivity for many days. A number of corrugated cartons with many fish species in them stood ready for shipment at the airport. A hand-sized *Serrasalmus spilopleura* was included in a plastic bag which held about two quarts of water. Shortly before the plane was ready to take off, one of the cartons was wet. Was it the Discus, which might have poked holes in the bags with their sharp spines? No. Naturally it was the Piranha in the shipment. A circular hole had been bitten out of the bag. I put it carefully in two bags placed one inside the other. The fish dashed angrily against the transparent walls and with a few bites wrecked the bags. A stream of water poured out. "Just wait!" I thought, "you haven't licked me yet, you beast!" I put a double dose of a sedative in

The head of *Serrasalmus hollandi* is much more elongated, the iris of the eyes silvery, but the sharp teeth, even if they are not backed up with the strong musculature of other species, are well able to inflict a painful wound on a careless fisherman when he takes one off of a hook. By its small size and beauty, this species is well adapted for the home aquarium. But care must always be taken if several specimens are kept together, because they might injure each other if something is not to their liking.

The head of *Serrasalmus rhombeus* is very similar to that of *S. hollandi*. Both species have a quite well-formed and somewhat larger mouth than the previous species. The teeth are somewhat smaller than with those species which have blunt, bulldog-like heads.

the water and put it in triple bags. There was no other way. It soon calmed down, and arrived safely and in good color.

I consider Piranhas as spiteful creatures. They *must* be fed with flesh; it can be seen in their eyes, in their movements and the stupid expressions on their faces. They have an urge to bite everything that can be grasped in their jaws. The species with the short, bulldog-like faces are certainly the nastiest, and are responsible for the many true but usually exaggerated stories about the "maneaters and hyenas" of the fresh waters.

Much more feared than the Piranhas in the Amazon River are the freshwater Stingrays (*Potamotrygidae*), which occur everywhere. They are commonly called "Raia" or "Araia" in Brazil. The Brazilians distinguish many species, and the scientific world confirms this. Stingrays lie motionless on the bottom, covered with sand or mud, invisible. They are not capable of eating anyone, but a wader could step on one, causing it to whip its tail about quickly and sink its spike, which is covered with barbs and an acid slime, into the foot, the leg or the calf. This injury is extremely painful, and if modern antibiotics cannot be resorted to, often does not heal for weeks.

We often hear on the Amazon and its mighty tributaries of dangers from large fishes which can threaten careless swimmers. Having fallen into the water, people are said to sometimes fail to come up to the surface. Amazon natives tell of powerful Catfish, the Piraiba (*Brachyplatystoma*), the "Shark of the freshwater", to which they attribute such accidents. Others speak of immense water-snakes, not paying much attention to a few yards added to the size. Piranhas cannot be held responsible for such mishaps, because according to the natives such things do not happen!

In the Amazon there is still another fish which attacks living humans. The Brazilians call it the Candirú, *Hemicetopsis candiru*. It is a parasitic fish which is very similar to the Lamprey. In its larval form it leads a parasitic existence in the gills of larger fishes, where it is found in great numbers. It gets its nourishment from the blood of its host. Candirús have the habit of remaining hidden in some place for days. When the brief dusk comes they swim out and attack bathers by biting out tiny bits of flesh and skin with their sharp little teeth. The uninitiated naturally think right away that they have been bitten by a Piranha. It is possible that these tiny, larva-like forms of the Candirú are in search of a suitable host. This may be the reason for their entry into the urethra of bathers, where they followed a stream of urine. It is

This is the most dreaded fish in the whole Amazon, the River Stingray. *Potamotrygidae* is the name of this family. Every time a native sees one of them on the bottom, he tries to spear it or kill it with his bush-knife or axe. Indians shoot them with bow and arrow, cut off their tails and throw the crippled fish back into the water. Then the freshwater hyenas come to their spoil. In a few seconds the Piranhas tear up and eat their defenseless prey!

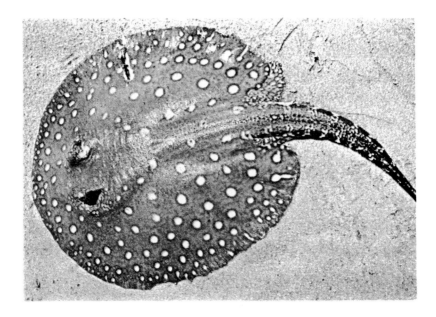

Serrasalmus rhombeus is called the "White Piranha" by Brazilian natives, and occurs in all Amazon bodies of water. It attains a length of 12 to 14 inches, making it one of the larger species. The body form is very similar to *S. hollandi*; a distinct marking is the black edge which encloses the tail and anal fin. Both species are humped slightly behind the head, and the line from the dorsal fin to the tail also shows some indentations. The color is silver with more dark gray markings than with *hollandi*.

my opinion that this larval form has a particularly developed surface sensitivity of the body which enables it to orient itself to the stream of water pushed out through the gills of a large fish and thereby find itself a host. Because the stream of urine might feel the same, it might be that the Candirús made a mistake and pushed their way into the urethral tract. There is a belief that Caudirús would follow the stream of urine of a person standing on the banks of a stream, to get into the urethral tract! The truth is, however, that Caudirus have been found in the drowned bodies of mammals. They can hollow out the entire body. If such a body is pulled ashore, the Candirús fall out from little holes which they have dug into the body. The Candirú is therefore a quite remarkable creature.

If one would take into consideration all the things which are said either truly or questionably about Amazon travels, the traveler could not even put his finger into the water without running the risk of losing it. For decades I have bathed in Piranha-infested waters without even thinking of any danger!

The Indians either spear the Stingray or shoot it with a bow and arrow. Often it takes several shots to be sure that the fish is dead.

As an excuse for many serious authors, it may be said that it is not always easy for a newcomer to distinguish where there is danger to be found and where there isn't! One must spend some time in a region before one can feel at home there.

The main nourishment of the Piranha is flesh. It can be assumed, however, that they also take other nourishment. Stomach contents of freshly-caught specimens are the only means of getting such information. I do not know if any such research has been made. I can only say from my own experience that Piranhas in nature are *always hungry*, and that they will accept other baits than meat, but not as readily.

Bathers in some Amazon streams are frightened by tiny fishes, Tetras with strong teeth which pick at all exposed parts of the human body, and dig into the skin with their tiny teeth. If a sensitive portion of skin is picked at, he might think it is a Piranha. But they do no harm to anyone; they do not have enough strength nor sharp enough teeth, but there are thousands of them. In some streams there are the always inquisitive *Exodon paradoxus*, in others there are small silvery Tetras of other species.

This beautiful Serrasalmus calmoni is a very rare Piranha.

Serrasalmus brandti is called the Pirambeba or Lake Piranha by the Brazilians. An almost oval fish with strongly compressed body, all silver. Pectoral, ventral and anal fins are yellowish brown. The entire fish has none of the typical appearance of the "dangerous" Piranhas, in spite of the fact that it belongs to the Serrasalmus genus. Body form and finnage serve to identify it as such, but the large eye, the much weaker construction of the head bones and the relatively small mouth make it much more similar to other more peaceful species which principally feed on vegetable matter. Still, this fish is a Piranha and has the sharp if smaller teeth of the genus. The scales are small, as are those of most Piranhas, and lie close to the body.

Catoprion mento, The Wimple Piranha, does not belong to the real Piranhas, and with it we show the way to the other species. However, in their native waters of Central Brazil, they are called *Bento Aleixo,* which is really a man's name, and the Brazilians consider it one of the Piranhas. Opinion is divided. Some say they are Piranhas, and others say that they are *Pacus,* that is, *Metynnis* and related species. Whatever the case might be, the name *Wimple Piranha* has become accepted and has its justification. *Catoprion mento* does not have the sharp teeth of the real Piranhas and one need have no worries, even for the larger inhabitants of the community aquarium. We show it on purpose as a transition from the real Piranhas to the other related fishes.

From my observations of Piranhas in their home waters, I had always believed that Piranhas spawned like most Cichlids in that they give parental care to the eggs and fry. Part of my reason for this assumption was that I had noticed that many Piranhas are much nastier and more ready to fight during their spawning period.

My observations have been borne out by at least two persons who have succeeded in spawning Piranhas in captivity, William P. Braker of the John G. Shedd public aquarium in Chicago and Kyle Swegles of the Rainbow Aquarium, also in Chicago. The species spawned were different (*Serrasalmus spilopleura* was spawned at the Shedd Aquarium, and *Serrasalmus nattereri* was spawned by Mr. Swegles), but in each case at least one parent defended and cared for the eggs and fry. The female sprays up to 5,000 adhesive eggs over the plants; the eggs hatch in about four days. As the fry grow they must be provided with enough food or they attack each other.

The head of the *Serrasalmus niger*, the Black Piranha.

The head of *Serrasalmus brandti* shows little similarity to the other Piranhas. The skull is not so enormously hard in bone construction as in the other species, the mouth is small, and so are the sharp teeth . . . still there is care required in handling them! But they would probably never be a menace to a bleeding human in the water . . . and they are definitely more shy!

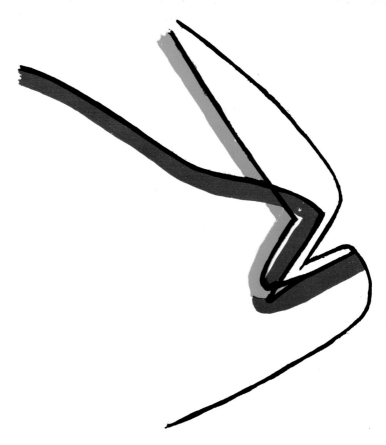

The head shapes of different Piranhas: In black is the outline of *Serrasalmus nattereri*. The green outline is *Catoprion mento*. The red outline is *Serrasalmus rhombeus*. Drawn by the author.

As soon as the rainy season sets in, which takes place in the upper reaches of the southern Amazon region towards December, there are young Piranhas to be found. In the lower reaches the water rises about two months later, and not until then are there young Piranhas to be found there. They hide between the blades of floating thickets of grass. It can easily happen at this time that such young Piranhas are caught along with other species. The next day one wonders why there are so many fins missing, until the villains are discovered.

Thirteen Red Piranhas caught by a little girl in half an hour!

Myloplus schomburgki, Schomburgk's Disc Tetra. With this fish we complete the transition from the Piranha species and find ourselves in the company of vegetarian fishes! They are at least basically vegetarian, if not entirely. There is no doubt that the *Pacus* as they are called in all Brazil are also carnivorous to a degree. Yes, some of them possess a very powerful set of jaws, with teeth that look human, and are capable of inflicting a severe wound. But the *Pacus* are known for their vegetarian habits and are preferred to the Piranhas when the natives are looking for food fish. *Pacus* are among the greatest delicacies among Brazilian food fishes, but Piranhas are often fished for and eaten, if there is nothing better to be had. *Myloplus schomburgki* is an attractive fish in spite of its silvery color, which becomes red on the gill-covers and pectoral fins. A dark vertical band adorns the body in the after half.

The head of *Catoprion mento* is particularly remarkable. The jutting lower jaw really looks like the shovel of a dredge. And still, it looks a great deal like a Piranha. Compare it with the head of *Serrasalmus rhombeus*, and it will be seen that the lower jaw of both species is of equal length. What gives the impression of a jutting lower jaw is the *shorter* upper jaw and head. With *Serrasalmus brandti* both the upper and lower jaws are shortened, giving the head of this Piranha species the appearance of a *Metynnis*. Do not judge the feeding habits of the Wimple Piranha by the shape of its head. In its native waters it eats everything and in my 45-gallon aquarium it gets anything from dried foods to tubifex worms, also eating from the bottom when the food sinks.

Fish endurance tests: Every year, shortly before the beginning of the rainy season, many fish have to undergo an endurance test for their lives. They gather in so-called Piracemas, tremendous fish migrations in schools which are miles long and often take weeks to pass. When they reach a waterfall, they must prove their ability to leap over it. They try once, twice, and often many times, but if they are not able to accomplish the leap and remain exhausted at the bottom, their fate awaits them in the form of large predatory fishes, the huge Catfishes, other species and our ill-famed Piranhas, and they soon find their way into the ever-hungry stomachs. Passing this "endurance test" is necessary for survival. Nature is more cruel than we humans, who protect the sick and weak, but there is also a law among animals that they should help each other. Where lies the truth?

If you ever go bathing in the Amazon or one of the beautiful tributaries and you are frightened by hundreds or thousands of little fishes swimming around you, these are often *Exodon paradoxus* or other less colorful species. If you presently feel that your entire body is being picked or nibbled, even in the most intimate places, don't tumble screaming out of the water. These are not Piranhas, but other harmless little fishes; they are mistaking you for a piece of candy which they have permission to nibble.

I like Piranhas and consider them good aquarium fishes. They are without a doubt interesting pets!

(1) Myers, "The Amazon and its Fishes" (Part V): A MONOGRAPH ON THE PIRANHA. Reprinted from the February 1949 issue of the Aquarium Journal, Stanford University.

This Piranha (*Serrasalmus?*) has a yellow throat and anal fin, plus some yellow in the tail as well. The body is silvery, with many tiny black spots. It is found in the blackwater tributaries of the upper reaches of the Amazon and attains the length of a man's hand, and although it could inflict a real injury nobody has any fear of them. Photo by Harald Schultz.

One of the most colorful of the deep-bodied Characins is *Myloplus schultzei*, a very timid fish that, like *Metynnis*, is a plant-eater. Photo by Harald Schultz.

This beautiful picture of *Serrasalmus nattereri* was made by Dr. Herbert R. Axelrod and shows why it is referred to as the Red Piranha. It is one of the species which is reputed to have inflicted injuries on humans, and the natives who collect fishes handle them very gingerly.

The following photographs depict an attack by a piranha on another fish in an aquarium. The victim in this case is *Pterophyllum scalare*, the angelfish. Photos by Folke Johnsson.

The piranha approaches its intended victim.

Having already bitten off part of the angelfish's finnage, the piranha turns the fish crosswise in its mouth for another bite.

The dead angelfish, with roughly half its body bitten away, drifts down to the bottom of the aquarium.

This is all that's left of the angelfish after just a few bites.

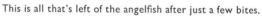

A species of pacu · Photo by Dr. Herbert R. Axelrod.

How Dangerous are Piranhas?

By Dr. George S. Myers

In the opinion of the public, the term "piranha" has come to signify a deadly, dangerous fish. In part, at least, this opinion is due to my "Monograph" of 1949, in which I gathered together a number of the harrowing tales that have been told of fatalities due to piranhas by travellers in piranha country . . . even to such eminent men as President Theodore Roosevelt. Since my "Monograph" appeared, however, there have been attempts to "debunk the piranha," and in the forefront of these have been not only the late Harald Schultz but also our publisher, Dr. Herbert R. Axelrod, both of whom have also travelled widely on South American rivers where piranhas are numerous. The opinions of these experienced men on piranhas deserve careful attention, and I have written this new article to do precisely that.

No intelligent person who is reasonably familiar with piranhas in South America has ever, so far as I know, said that piranhas always, or even usually, attack people swimming or wading in water in which these fishes are common. But the many people who have published accounts of fatalities caused by piranhas, some of them cited in my monograph, knew what they were talking about. They did not invent the stories they told. For example, I can mention the late General Candido Rondon, Brazil's famous explorer of the wilder rivers of his country, one of whose stories I translated and included in my "Monograph." Few people ever had more years of experience in piranha country than General Rondon, and he had a healthy respect for these fishes.

At the same time, Harald Schultz also had years of experience along Brazilian rivers, as an anthropologist studying the Indians and as a collector of fishes. He made a considerable point of the fact that the Indians are bathing in the rivers all the time, without showing fear of piranhas, and of the additional fact that during thousands of miles of travel on Brazilian rivers he never came across a case of serious injury by piranhas.

I do not doubt Schultz's word in any way. Although I have not had nearly as long experience in piranha country as Schultz had, my own lesser experience entirely agrees with his. The people who live along the rivers show little fear of piranhas, and specific cases of attack by piranhas are very hard to locate, even when you try to do so.

It would be well to point out, however, that hundreds of thousands of people throughout the world often bathe and swim along ocean beaches where sharks are known to occur without being attacked. Most such bathers certainly show no fear of sharks when they enter the water. One could travel along thousands of miles of such beaches without ever finding anybody who had been bitten by a shark, or even knew anybody who had ever been bitten. But anybody who believes that sharks do not attack and kill people is simply out of his mind.

In truth, this comparison of the dangerous nature of sharks and piranhas is a very useful one for emphasizing the points I wish to make. Moreover, the changing beliefs of both naturalists and the public about sharks during the past fifty years illustrates beautifully what is now happening in regard to beliefs about piranhas.

Previous to about 1925 or 1930 it was taken for granted that most of the kinds of larger sharks of coastal inshore waters, especially in warmer regions, were dangerous to man. Accounts of people bitten, killed or eaten by sharks were numerous enough so that people did not doubt them, even though there had been little special study of shark habits and no concerted attempt to gather careful statistics of shark attacks had ever been made. For example, I recall from my boyhood the year (1915 or 1916) when there were a number of shark attacks, and some fatalities, along the coasts of the Middle Atlantic States. There were shark articles in the supplements of the Sunday newspapers and one great white shark was caught with parts of a man in its stomach. Attendance at the bathing beaches of New York and New Jersey plummeted that summer.

But the memory of the public, and of some scientists, is short. By the mid-1920's, that prestigious naturalist, the late Dr. William Beebe, had transferred his attention from birds and other terrestrial animals to undersea creatures. Following the lead of Dr. W. H. Longley of Goucher College in Baltimore, Beebe did a great deal of shallow-water diving in tropical waters. Modern SCUBA gear had not been invented, and Beebe, like Longley, used a helmet to which air was pumped through a hose from a boat on the surface. Of course, Beebe observed many sharks and soon discovered the basic underwater fact, already known to Longley, that most sharks will approach and inspect an underwater diver but rarely or never attempt to attack him unless he is thrashing about and in evident difficulty. And if they do approach too closely, they can usually be discouraged by the diver becoming motionless, or giving the shark a hard poke on the nose or in the eye with a sharp stick or long knife.

Beebe published many books on undersea life, culminating with his *Half-Mile Down*, which described the first really deep dive ever made successfully by man in the Barton-Beebe bathysphere[1] off Bermuda. In several of his books there is the recurring theme that sharks are not really dangerous to man unless spurred on by "unnatural movements" such as thrashing or splashing about. And Beebe was believed. He had "debunked the shark," and his views on sharks were widely accepted.

Then came World War II. Hundreds of men from ships sunk or aircraft shot down in the tropical Pacific saw comrades, especially but not necessarily injured men, attacked and eaten by sharks. These men had never read Beebe but nobody could debunk sharks so far as they were concerned! It was in the first half of the 1940's, during the war, that the first extensive studies of shark habits, and of possible shark repellent substances, were begun, by the U.S. Navy. Those studies have by now vastly expanded until dozens of shark-study centers are now operating. Extensive combing of publications of all sorts for mention of shark attacks and interviews with observers or survivors have now produced bulging files of information, and the behavior of sharks is constantly being studied. Many species of sharks are now known to be very dangerous to men in the water, and human death by shark bite is authenticated for many of them. The naive era of Beebe's shark-debunking is now blotted out by stacks of precise information.

It seems to me that the debunking of the dangers of piranhas by Harald Schultz is in many ways closely parallel to Beebe's debunking of sharks. The average person who goes bathing on a Florida beach or on the banks of the Amazon still does so without being afraid of attack by fishes, sharks or piranhas. But he knows (or should know) that there are deadly dangerous fishes in those waters and that he had better not go into the water in places the local people tell him are dangerous.

Another comparison that may be useful is one with lions in East Africa. Few people are so foolish as to believe that the lion is not a deadly dangerous animal. If any are that foolish they should read the story of the two lions of Tsavo, who halted construction of a railroad in East Africa by killing and

---

[1] My own salute to Beebe's great achievement was the following:

Down, down, down, to the bottom of the sea—
Visit Davy Jones's Locker! Won't you come along with me?
We'll see the wonders of the deep; there is no cause for fear,
For my name is William Beebe, and this is my bathysphere.

G.S.M.

eating dozens of the workmen.[2] Yet enough is now known about lions and their habits so that tourists (who must remain in their cars) may observe and photograph them under very carefully laid-down conditions. Of course lions are deadly! *So are piranhas.*

Almost everybody who has travelled in piranha country has noted the fact that bathing is done in many places in the rivers without danger. As I have mentioned, Schultz makes much of this fact. However, his story would be a great deal more persuasive if, at each place where he observed the local people bathing, he had inquired as to whether there were other local places where nobody bathed because of piranhas. My own experience, and that of others who have written on piranhas, is that the people of almost every riverside community know of local places where bathing or swimming would invite attack by piranhas. Of course they bathe in the safe places and take that so much as a matter of course that the question of safe versus unsafe places is never mentioned, unless somebody inquires very specifically

Then there is the problem of the behavior of the piranhas themselves, a subject that has never really been carefully studied, so far as I know. As I emphasized in my "Monograph," many or most Characidae (the family to which the piranhas belong) are attracted, like sharks, to disturbances in the water, whereas most fishes are frightened by such disturbances. The kicking and splashing of a man swimming rapidly on the surface will attract piranhas, whereas a man swimming slowly is much less likely to attract them. But aside from such things, we do not know much.

It is notable that the village bathing places, where the women and children wade in and wash themselves or their clothes, are usually shallow, not much over knee or waist deep, and that there is more wading than swimming, at least among adults. In my experience, adult piranhas are not commonly found in such shallow water. Two things in particular are to be noted in this regard. Swimming in the deeper water off such bathing places is not often seen. It is my belief that generations upon generations of local natives have more or less fixed the bathing places that are not dangerous and established the custom of not entering water of over waist depth. Second, it is particularly in such shallow places, especially ones with a sandy bottom, that sting rays are most commonly found. With bathing restricted by age-old custom to such places, probably originally because larger piranhas are few or absent, it is wholly to be expected that the people show less fear of rare piranha bites than of the far commoner, agonizingly painful wounds made by stingrays. Among less advanced people everywhere, custom that was originally established to forestall a definite danger often persists when the original danger is no longer clearly remembered.

[2] These two lions were finally hunted down and shot. They are mounted and on exhibition in Field Museum in Chicago, which publishes a booklet giving their story.

Certain things about piranha behavior are quickly discovered and absorbed by people, even by visitors who do not stay long. For example, I have stood knee deep in a stream in Amazonian Colombia surrounded by a school of smaller piranhas cutting up slightly smaller fishes and eating them. No piranhas I ever saw were more savage. They swam around and dashed between my legs like lightning, and the clipped-off halves of the fishes they were feeding on floated all about. Yet I was not in the slightest danger and had no fear of them. My legs were, to them, no more than stationary posts in the water, and they were intent on eating the smaller fishes. Yet I thought at the time that had I raised one of my pale, waterlogged toes above the brown sand which covered them, it would probably have been severely bitten. I simply waited for the piranhas to finish off the other fishes and depart before I moved.

Another thing to remember is that there are relatively few big cities along the rivers where piranhas are abundant. Nearly all the settlements are relatively small and it is a rare settlement in which there is a resident medical doctor. Roads, except for short ones to a few nearby places, do not exist and nearly all travel is by boat on the river. A great many of the people cannot read or write. In such a region no statistics of piranha attacks are kept. Any which result fatally may never be known except to a few people. Any attack on an isolated boatman who accidentally overturns his canoe is very likely to be fatal, and all his friends ever know is that the man vanished in some way and never came home. Along more rivers than may seem possible, no one except sparse Indian tribes lives. Under such conditions, a man such as Harald Schultz may travel very long distances without ever hearing of a single piranha attack. Yet there may have been a number of them within a reasonable distance of every one of his stopping places, if one had a complete local record for the preceding twenty-five years.

No! Neither sharks nor lions nor rattlesnakes nor piranhas automatically kill off a person who enters their habitat. But anyone who says that any of these is not a deadly dangerous animal is very foolish. And I should still prefer to face, in the water, a large shark of almost any of the dangerous species than a school of piranhas in a South American river! You can't poke a school of piranhas in the eye!

I think I should include here a brief statement about the fears expressed by certain government agencies in the United States about the possible accidental introduction of piranhas into United States waters. No piranhas could survive the cold, snowy winters in most parts of the country. They are essentially tropical fishes. However, some parts of the United States (e.g., Florida and southern California) have very mild winters, in which tropical fishes survive the winter in outdoor ponds. The Amazonian cichlid *Astronotus* is now firmly established in southern Florida waters, where it is becoming common. Moreover, the best known of the truly dangerous piranhas

(Serrasalmus nattereri) occurs naturally all the way from tropical northern South America to the Paraná delta not far from Buenos Aires, where the winters are often far colder than those of Florida. This species could almost certainly become established if introduced into our southernmost states. Such introduction would be a catastrophe!

Finally, piranhas once fully established in a river or lake would be virtually impossible to eradicate. The so-called rotenone "fish poisons," which merely suffocate but do not really poison fishes, are widely used in North America by fishery biologists to eradicate all the fishes in a lake or stream in order to introduce new kinds more successfully. (This reprehensible practice is now being increasingly frowned upon by conservationists.) In smaller quantities, rotenone is also used by ichthyologists to collect fish specimens for preservation in formaldehyde or alcohol for studies of classification. I have used rotenone to collect study-specimens in many parts of South America. My experiences indicate that piranhas are strongly resistant to rotenone. Other fishes are always killed in large numbers, but fishing with rotenone rarely produces a single piranha, even in places where many piranhas can be seen in the water—or even dashing through the clouds of rotenone.

Cambridge, Mass.—*November* 1971.

Postscript *by The Publisher,* Dr. Herbert R. Axelrod.

There is a great deal of interest in piranhas amongst aquarists. They have been bred in captivity and have captured the imagination of the masses as California officials have publicized their effective campaign to destroy every piranha within the state's borders.

As Chairman of the Exotic Fish Committee of the American Fisheries Society at the present time (November, 1971), it is my committee's task to recommend to the Congress of the United States, and other regulatory bodies, the consensus amongst scientists pertaining to the introduction of all foreign (thus "exotic") species, including but not limited to the piranha.

When such experts on piranhas, and fish behavior in general, as George Myers and Harald Schultz vary so greatly, I thought it might be well to dig a bit deeper. With this in mind I went to Venezuela where, with one of Prof. Myers' students, Dr. Agustin Fernandez-Yepez, I visited the Rio Aguarro, a piranha-infested river. I tested many theories and came away with the following report:

1. The Rio Aguarro had piranhas *(Pygopristes antoni)* in every part which was at least one meter (about 40 inches) deep. No piranhas were seen in shallow waters.

2. They are easily caught on fish bait, fruit bait (in the form of a piece of ripe mango) or decaying meat.

3. Piranhas did not hit a series of lures; but *Metynnis* did.

4. When I poisoned the area, I killed thousands of fishes, including many cichlids and characins. I did not kill one piranha.

5. When I swam across the lake (foolishly), I was not attacked by piranha, nor any other fish, even though I had caught several dozen piranhas on hook and line within an hour of my swim.

6. When I dove down with a face mask, or floated on the surface with a snorkel, the piranhas stayed far away from me.

7. Using a large seine, I caught many piranhas on my first sweep with the net; I caught none with successive swoops of the net.

8. The analysis of the stomach contents of the piranha of the Rio Aguarro contained mostly pieces of small fishes.

These were my observations on the *Pygopristes antoni* piranha from the Rio Aguarro. I agree with everything that Harold Schultz says about their behavior and I agree with everything Dr. Myers writes about their potential danger, but I have personally dived from my boat in almost every major river system in Brazil, out in the deep water, and I never saw a piranha, though I caught many of them in the deep open parts of the river. Of course I am afraid to be attacked by piranhas, just as I am afraid to be attacked by a shark when I swim in the ocean, or being bitten by a dog when I see one, but the chances of being attacked by piranhas in a full river (as contrasted to a dried-out river where the piranhas might be starving) are so negligible in my opinion that aside from a **"warning—piranhas"** sign I wouldn't be afraid to go for a swim anyplace in a full natural river.

However, as chairman of a committee charged with making specific recommendations, I must advise against the importation and release of piranhas in natural waters, for I'd rather make the mistake of prohibiting the importation and release of a non-dangerous species than advocating the release and importation of a fish which should not have been allowed in. It's not just worth the risk and I must, therefore, support Dr. Myers.

PUBLISHER'S NOTE

The following gallery of drawings by the famed Venezuelan ichthyologist Agustin Fernandez-Yepez shows the piranhas (*caribes*) of Venezuela along with their local names in Spanish. The drawings were not made to be analytically exact and serve merely as a guide to shape and markings so that the hobbyist or customs inspector can recognize whether or not a fish is a piranha. These drawings were not made under the supervision of the editor, who takes no responsibility for their correctness.

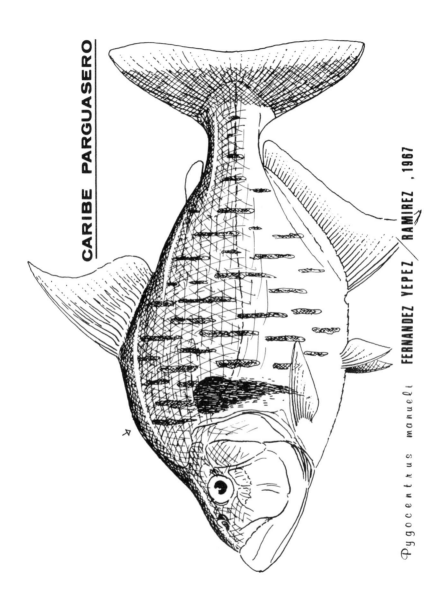

CARIBE PARGUASERO

Pygocentrus manueli **FERNANDEZ YEPEZ / RAMIREZ , 1967**

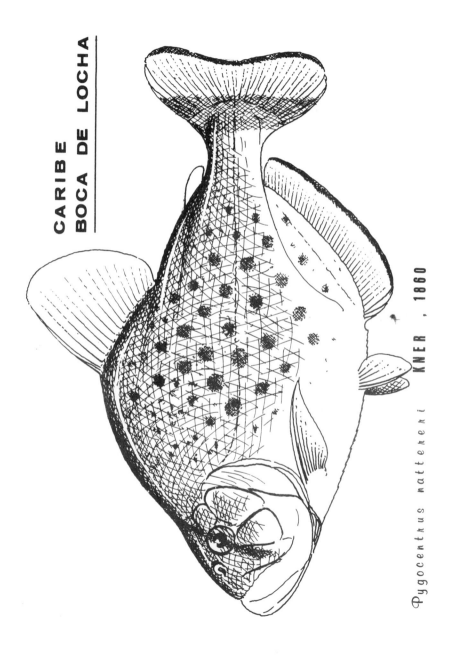

CARIBE
BOCA DE LOCHA

Pygocentrus nattereri KNER , 1860

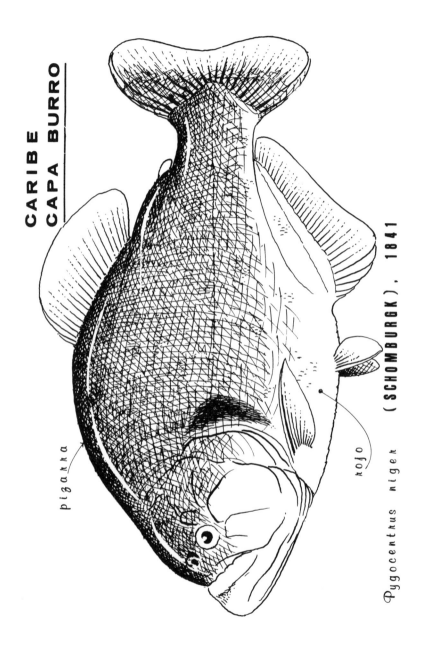

CARIBE
CAPA BURRO

Pygocenthus niger (SCHOMBURGK), 1841

piyarra

rojo

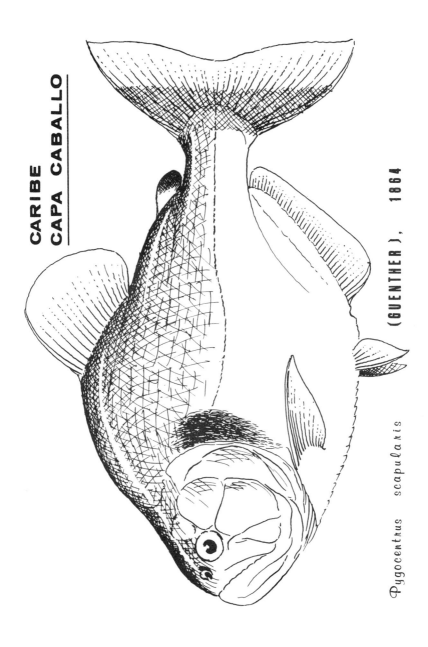

CARIBE
CAPA CABALLO

Pygocentrus scapularis (GUENTHER), 1864

CARIBE CORTADOR

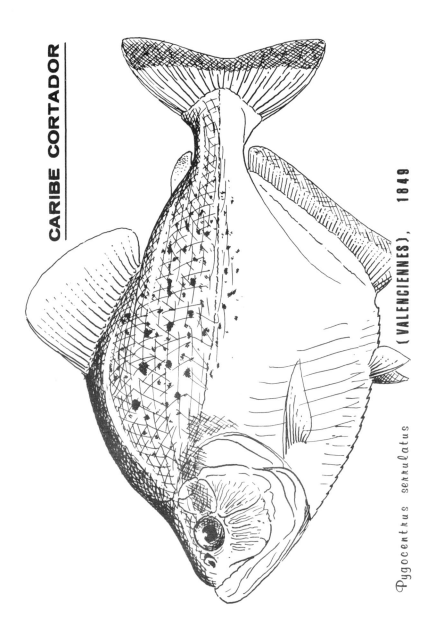

Pygocentrus serrulatus (VALENCIENNES), 1849

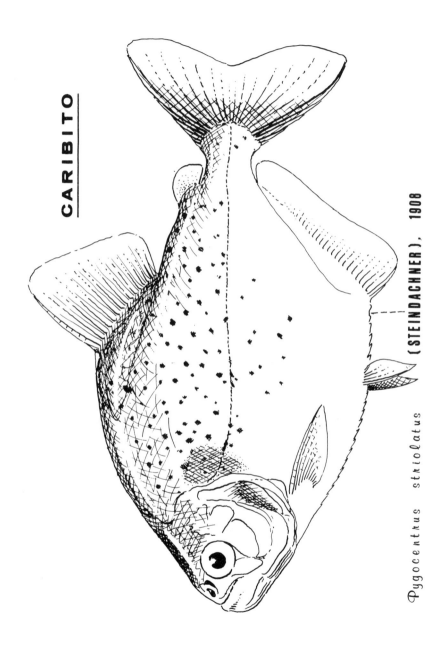

CARIBITO

Pygocentrus striolatus **(STEINDACHNER), 1908**

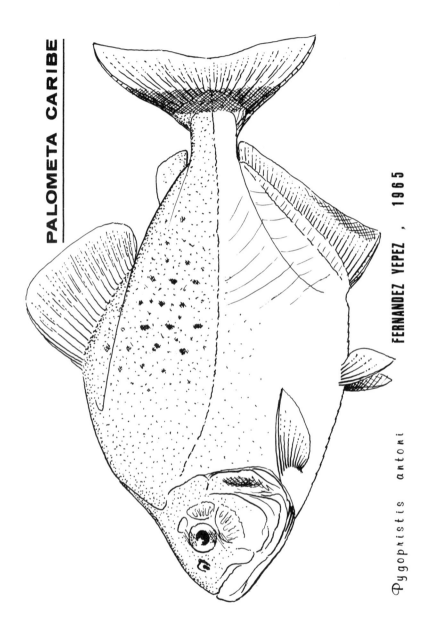

PALOMETA CARIBE

FERNANDEZ YEPEZ , 1965

Pygopristis antoni

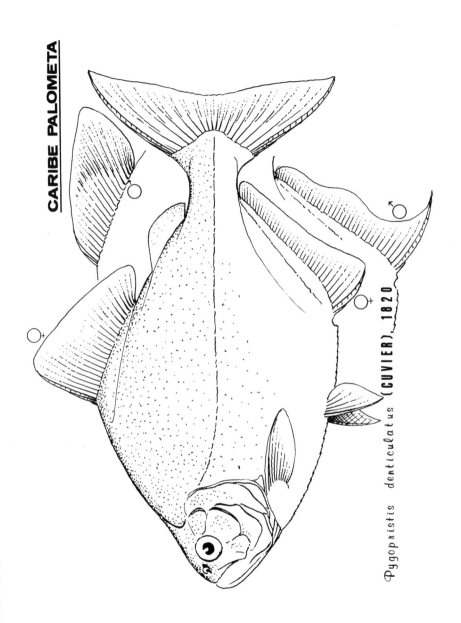

CARIBE PALOMETA

Pygopristis denticulatus **(CUVIER), 1820**

113

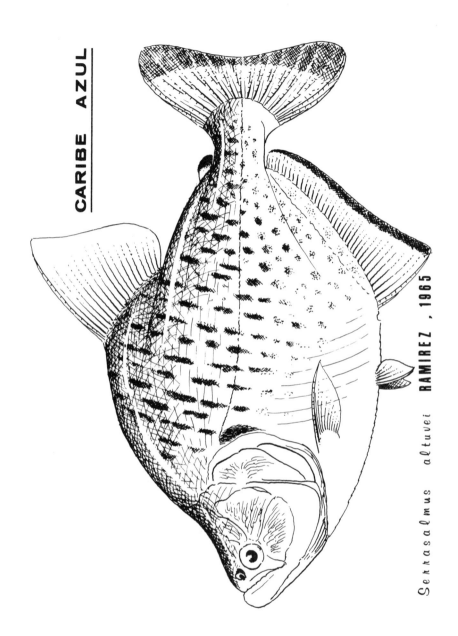

CARIBE AZUL

Serrasalmus altuvei RAMIREZ , 1965

114

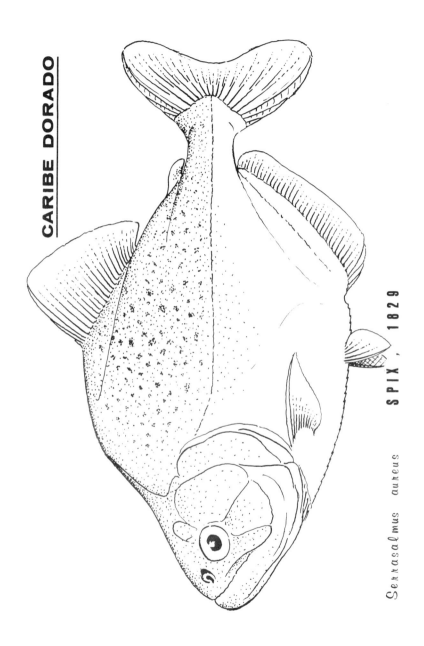

CARIBE DORADO

Serrasalmus aureus **SPIX, 1829**

115

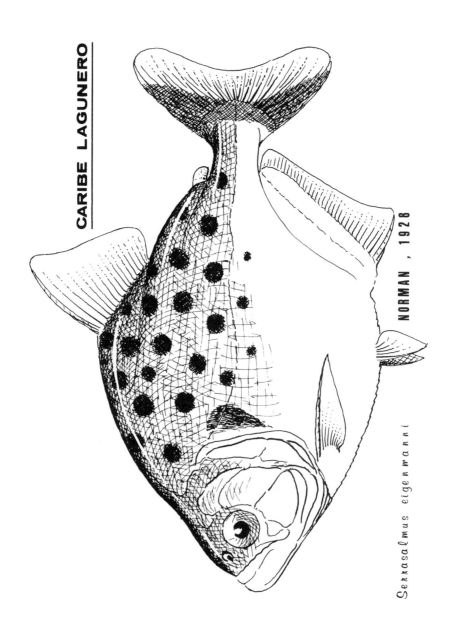

CARIBE LAGUNERO

NORMAN , 1928

Serrasalmus eigenmanni

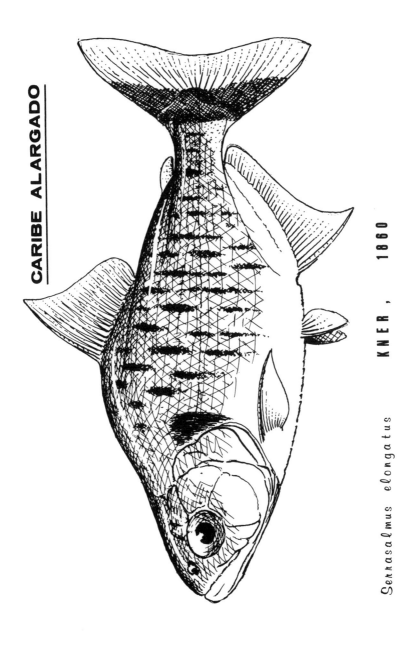

CARIBE ALARGADO

Serrasalmus elongatus KNER, 1860

117

CARIBE MONDONGUERO

Serrasalmus fernandezi FERNANDEZ YEPEZ , 1965

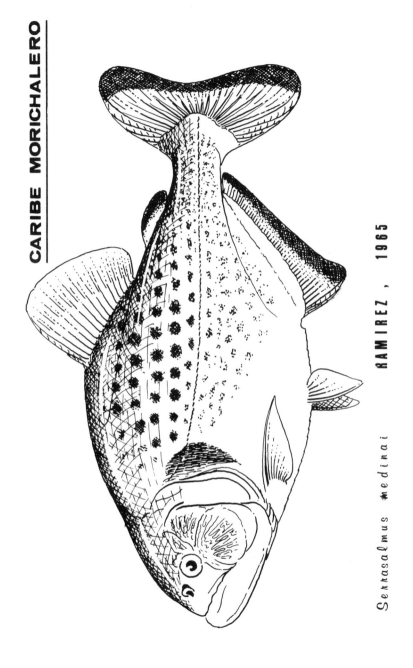

CARIBE MORICHALERO

Serrasalmus medinai **RAMIREZ , 1965**

119

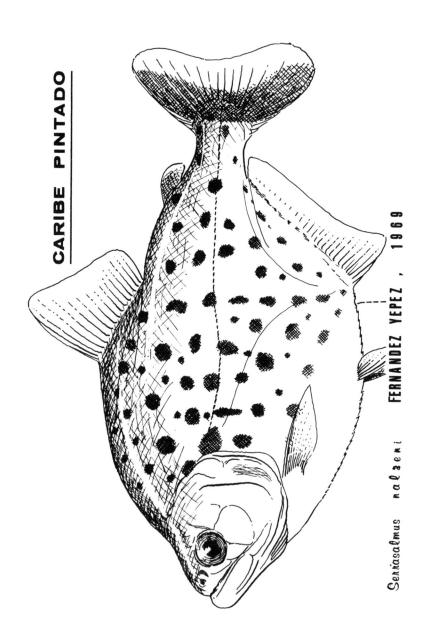

CARIBE PINTADO

Serrasalmus nalseni FERNANDEZ YEPEZ , 1969

CARIBE PINCHE

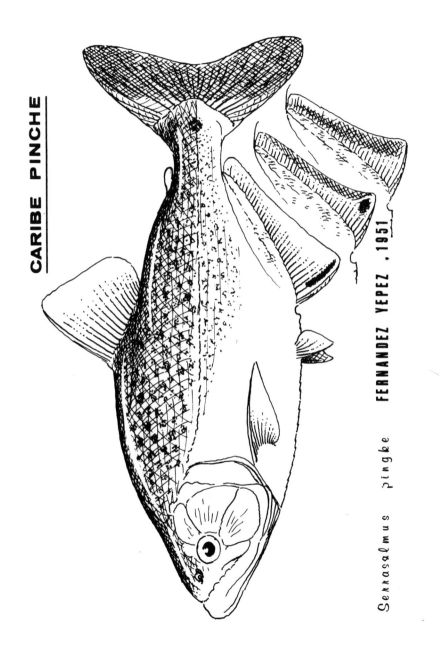

Serrasalmus pingke   FERNANDEZ YEPEZ , 1951

CARIBE AMARILLO
(caribe ojo rojo)

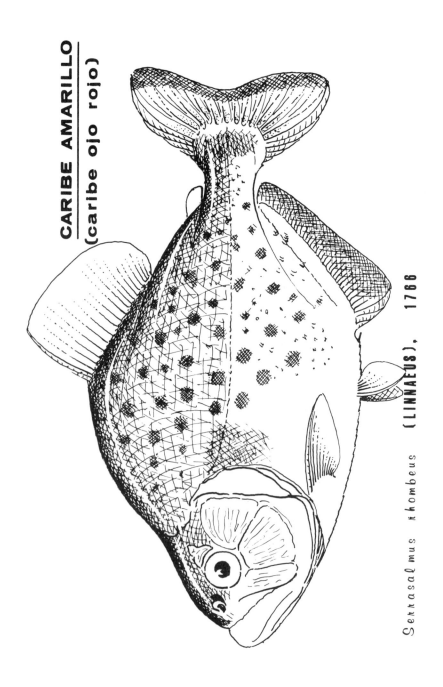

Serrasalmus rhombeus (LINNAEUS), 1766

CARIBE CACHAMERO

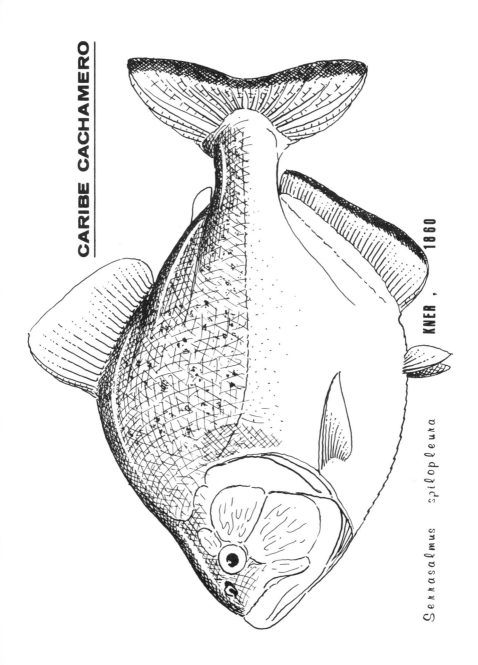

Serrasalmus spilopleura

KNER, 1860

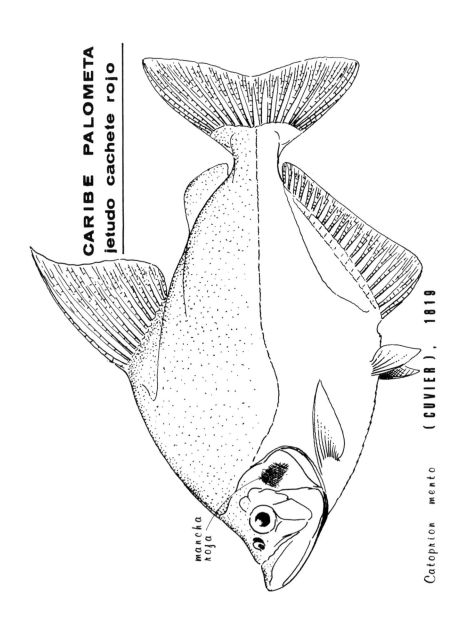

CARIBE PALOMETA
jetudo cachete rojo

mancha roja

Catoprion mento (CUVIER), 1819

124

INDEX
Entries listed in **bold** type refer to illustrations.